BUSINESS PLANS to game plans

A Practical System for Turning Strategies into Action

revised edition

JAN B. KING

WILEY

JOHN WILEY & SONS, INC.

To my wonderful son Kraig Rand King, my joy and inspiration.

PREFACE

According to the U.S. Department of Commerce, only one in five businesses remains open five years after its inception. The common denominator in these failures is entrepreneurs who underestimate the amount of time and money it will take to make the business succeed. On the surface, this seems to suggest that businesses fail from a lack of resources. In fact, the actual cause is the failure to plan the *right* resources to make the business succeed, grow, and thrive. In this book, I provide you with the strategies and tools you need to learn how to do things right and how to do the right things.

During the nine years I was CEO of Merritt Publishing, we faced a wider variety of challenges than I could have imagined, and I draw upon my experiences throughout the book. I needed wisdom and luck, but also accurate data and definitive analyses to make good decisions for the company. Because I couldn't find the diagnostic tools I needed to chart the best course for my company, I created them as I went along. I was able to double my company's revenues and improve profitability by an even greater factor during my tenure.

The tools in this book will help you lead your company from your business plan to your game plan. The worksheets and exercises provide you with the kind of critical data you need to run your business successfully. They'll help you find the answers you need to:

- Shift the corporate culture so employees are more accountable for their job performance.
- Better measure those areas that drive your business.
- Create an infrastructure that supports growth.
- Know what you need to grow your company: more capital, more people, or new products.

- Determine if sales are as profitable as they could be.

- Develop and launch new products while minimizing your risk.

I wrote this book to help other owners and managers learn what I learned but in a much shorter time. Each chapter starts with a discussion of relevant concepts and issues, including case studies. The case studies make the point that all of these disciplines, whether marketing or finance, are interrelated. In other words, in times of great opportunity and growth as well as in times of business downturns and consolidation, solutions to problems come from all segments of your business working together. Therefore, I argue that all employees should see the results of all areas of your business, not just those that directly relate to them. This discussion is followed by a series of progressive exercises and worksheets, with directions on how to use them entitled "Making It Happen," and questions to be asked about your data once you collect it, entitled "Reality Check," to help you discover your strengths and weaknesses.

These worksheets are intended to be used; please copy them freely. Distribute them to as many employees as you think useful. You may want to visit our web site at janbking.com to find electronic copies of the worksheets and enter your own data on your computer. Whatever medium you use, the object of these worksheets remains the same: to help you develop your business plan and your game plan and finally to help you take control of your business—and to make it an enduring success.

It takes more than data to run a successful business, and this book will also help you develop simple ways to determine whether your business is flourishing or failing—while there is still time to make mid-course corrections. Another crucial ingredient for success that I'll stress throughout is developing the ability to inspire key staff to commit to the business's success. In part, this comes from communicating your vision at every opportunity to your employees, suppliers, and your network of business associates. You also will do well to listen to those employees who work directly with customers. They're in the best position to convey what your customers want from the business.

Involving your employees fully in the business can have profound results. I'll come back to this throughout the book. It's hard for me to imagine this now, but before I became CEO, I felt no direct connection to the financial well-being of the company I worked for. My bonus aside, it didn't occur to me to ask about the financial statements, and anyway, my job description said nothing about "making" money. Nor would I have been interested enough to ask what our financial statements meant had I seen them.

One of the things I learned when I took over the reins was that every employee must understand the financial implications of each decision. Gradually, as I involved my employees more and more in the company's finances, I found that in effect management needed to become more flexible and self-directed as well.

If you choose the path of including your employees in the management of the company, you will be doing something for which little precedent exists. You will find little information in the management literature to support you or guide you in the difficulties you will encounter. Despite a host of experts who talk about *empowerment*, few practical models exist.

Empowerment should mean imparting the wisdom and sharing the tools with which to do a job successfully. In doing so, you may be giving employees more responsibility than they want. Before you decide whether to involve your employees more fully, you'll have to ask questions such as:

- By giving more decision-making responsibility to employees are you avoiding your responsibility for managing the company—and isn't that your job, not theirs?

- Are you passing the buck to your employees for decision making? This is something like the fundamental problem with democracy—are less capable, informed, and trained people making decisions?

- Is decision making too decentralized? Do you end up with "decisions by committee?"

- Are you making peoples' lives more complicated and more difficult? Are you creating chaos instead of clarity?

The answers aren't simple but struggling with these issues and allowing employees to struggle with their own problems was the only course of action I was satisfied with. In my case, involving my employees with the governance of the company enabled us to create an environment with minimal rules, much open communication and sharing of information, and high-quality thinking. We celebrated our successes as a group and jointly took responsibility for our defeats. I am proud to have enabled this organization to reach its potential, and throughout the book, I'll introduce ways to involve your employees in every decision.

Running a business is one of the most challenging, potentially rewarding jobs in the world. Devote yourself to doing it well and use this book as a resource to chart your course.

Finally, I want to acknowledge some of the many people whose help and support were invaluable in the writing of this book. My gratitude to the editors at John Wiley & Sons for their advice and counsel. Thanks to all the business owners, managers, and consultants who agreed to be interviewed for the case studies in this book. Thanks to TEC (The Executive Committee) an organization of CEOs whose members, facilitators, and resource speakers have consistently challenged my thinking about business and made me focus on my own business. Thanks to the clients and staff of the Small Business Development Centers. You are all an inspiration, showing what can be done with scarce resources but a determination to succeed. And personal thanks to Jim Walsh, Walt Sutton, Harriet Glicklich, and Andy Lipkis for being models of how to live rich, full, and profoundly meaningful lives.

JAN B. KING

CONTENTS

PART I

CREATE YOUR VISION

1

MOVING FROM VISION TO ACTION

There is nothing in a caterpillar that tells you it's going to be a butterfly.

—Buckminster Fuller

I call this book *Business Plans to Game Plans* because it takes you from your business plan, that is, what you share with those outside your business, like investors, to your game plan, which is how you really run the business, and what you share with your employees.

As a business-planning consultant, I have written countless business plans. While many of them received the funding they were hoping to attract, a number of these businesses failed in the first several years or never got out of the planning stage. In fact, a few of the entrepreneurs I worked with expected the business plan to be a blueprint for how to run the business. They couldn't be more wrong.

Here is one major difference between the business plan and the game plan: A business plan is written to impress others with how much you already know so that they can decide if they want to invest money in your venture. Entrepreneurs need to build their weaknesses into some sort of plan so that they don't neglect to take care of them. It's acceptable to admit you don't have all of the answers in the game plan, but you never see any such admissions in a successful business plan.

Business plans do not include implementation instructions, because the writers of business plans focus on accomplishment. They write as if once you dream the dream, it magically becomes reality. They don't write about the hard part—that is, the work it takes to gain success.

INVENTING YOUR COMPANY

Implementing a business plan and a game plan takes hard work. It takes wisdom, discipline, courage, an eye for detail, and, most of all, persistence. It also requires an outward focus and an inward focus. You must set goals, communicate them, review them, monitor their realization, and stick to them when other people might abandon them. Your hard work will pay off, and with the tools I offer in this book, you can make your company a success.

I know how hard it can be to run a business. In 1990, I suddenly found myself running a publishing company where I'd worked for seven years. In a matter of weeks, I had to grapple with a wide range of management problems; with little relevant experience and no formal business education, I had to learn to take control.

My company had been in business since 1957. I came to it as a writer and editor, then as the company's editorial director—a solid middle management position. The company also had the good fortune to be so profitable and cash rich in its formative years that there had been little need to project or monitor sales or expenses, cash or profit. The downside of this was that very little had been done to set expectations or monitor performance. It was hard to tell how well we were doing at any given time—or how well we would do in the future.

By the time I began running the company, we were no longer cash rich and our markets were changing dramatically, primarily due to new technologies that both made entry into our markets much easier and changed traditional distribution methods dramatically. Without cash to invest in our own growth, I knew we would not survive over the long term.

We had no choice but to reinvent the company. In effect, we were a 40-year-old start-up. We needed a business plan and we needed a game plan. We had to translate a new vision into action.

In the months that followed, I realized that the key to our survival was to get a handle on where our cash was going and reduce our expenses. We needed to change the corporate culture from a happy family business to one where accountability played a significant role. Last, but maybe most importantly, we also had to have a better understanding of what our business was fundamentally, who we were selling products to and what they would want in the future, and which of our over 200 products were profitable.

Challenge #1: Finance

Although my background was not in finance (or in business), company invoices were much like the bills I paid at home: I knew we paid rent, utilities, insurance, and salaries. I also knew that we paid for the products we produced and their marketing. Then, there were many other items like the outside professionals, computers, and miscellaneous items like office supplies.

Over several weeks, we sorted these invoices from the just-ended fiscal year into categories that seemed to make sense and covered all the types of invoices we found. In questioning people about what each individual invoice pertained to, we found—to our amazement—that many bills had been paid for services we no longer received. This was particularly true for maintenance contracts on equipment we no longer owned. Once the accounting department had been told to expect a particular bill each month, they continued to pay it without question. Many bills are addressed to accounts payable, and paid without anyone else ever seeing them. We cut about $77,000 in expenses simply by questioning old invoices. That was the first step to taking control of the business and to the development of the worksheets in this book.

Challenge #2: Corporate Culture

My next challenge was in determining employee accountability on a larger scale. How could I hold the employees accountable if they did not know how the company was doing? Because my company was (at the time) partially employee owned, the answer was to share financial information with everyone. I've heard the arguments against this kind of openness, the most compelling of which was that competitors could use this information against you. However, I took employee ownership seriously and expected everyone at the company to help run our business. I couldn't expect others to do what I couldn't do myself—namely, to run a business without knowing those numbers by which we measure success or failure. Too, I shared financial documents with my employees in the hope that they would see how the numbers sprang from their own work. I wanted my employees to grasp the numbers as proof of the importance to the company of everything they did.

In short, I gave my employees access to the financial statements and other documents to help them make intelligent decisions about their work. I educated them about what the numbers meant in the expectation that they would use those numbers not just to gauge our success, but to guide their actions. I discovered the remarkable power you harness by doing this. I discuss in further detail how to empower your employees to understand their impact on the bottom line in Chapter 2.

Informing your employees can have a profound impact on all aspects of your business. Of all the memories I have of the early years, the one I value most came after I started circulating the financial and operational reports. At a rather ordinary operations meeting, an employee suggested that we reduce inventory, saying that this would increase our cash position going into the critical months of our year.

It was an extraordinary moment. Financial consultants talk to boards of directors for hours about inventory accountancy, but on his own, this employee figured out that a tight inventory meant more available cash for us. His comprehension signaled to me that my openness with the numbers had paid off. Moreover, this episode reminded me that when I had been a nonmanagement employee, I had never stopped to think about the impact of inventory on cash in the bank. This is the subject of Chapter 5.

Challenge #3: Marketing and Sales

Like many entrepreneurs, the founder of my company hadn't believed in sharing financial information with his employees. We received monthly sales reports, and the bonus program for managers depended on profits. I knew that profits depended on sales, and sales interested me insofar as it pleased me to see that the books I wrote actually sold. However, sales seemed magical to me; I had no way to predict them. More important, I didn't think I could affect them in any immediate way. I eagerly awaited the accountant's proclamation at the end of each year—to find out whether I'd get a bonus. I had no clue how I personally could impact sales.

When I became CEO, I found that trying to boost sales was hard, but I developed a number of steps you can take to make your forecasts more accurate, as I'll discuss throughout the book. In my case, I did the following things, all of which are covered in the book:

- I listed all the products we sold, from the biggest revenue earner to the least; I then made the same list using our customer data. I was eventually able to calculate the profitability for each product and each customer. This became my company's guide as to which products to sell most aggressively, and to which customers, as I'll discuss in Chapter 4.

- We discontinued products where we were unable to reduce costs or raised prices where we thought the market would allow it. Some programs worked well, others didn't work at all.

- We closely tracked all our marketing efforts and duplicated those that worked well in tests, as discussed in Chapter 6.

- We constantly tested new approaches; and we worked out kinks in marketing, production, and fulfillment.

- We refined and simplified our corporate vision and mission statements, as covered later in this chapter.

- We began to develop offshoots of our most successful products.

- We paid close attention to what our largest customers liked and didn't like and constantly improved our existing products. This resulted in a doubling of our sales in a few short years.

- We simplified our reports and key indicators, focusing them on things of importance and ridding them of everything else. These had started out unnecessarily complex, based on imprecise formulas and assumptions. The longer we used them, the more basic they became. I cover this area in Chapter 3 on understanding the numbers.

- Finally, personally, I had to train myself to understand how the business was doing on a daily basis. Equally important, I had to make sure the other employees knew how the business was doing so that they would work toward the objectives we developed. I discuss tactics for motivating your employees and communicating your goals in Chapters 7 and 8.

Challenge #4: Creating a Future for the Company

After I had been CEO for almost two years, the founder of the company passed away, leaving us without a plan for a change in ownership. The company was already 40 percent employee owned, and we had decided together to take it to 100 percent. Some of the money had to be generated internally, so we had to become more profitable. Some of the money had to be borrowed, which forced us to put together a written business and marketing plan.

Creating a goal like this one generates unbeatable motivation. Suddenly, our definition of winning was more similar to an athletic game—there was a real dollar number we had to meet or beat to win. This was the genesis of the game plans I've used. They gave people real reasons to hold tight on expenses, and develop new products—reasons that people could get excited about for personal reasons. Every person working at the company had a reason to step up to the plate.

We decided to set up committees that would meet weekly and make sure the plans we made were being implemented. The two major committees monitored profitability (mostly from the revenue side) and expenses. Reporting to these committees were other subcommittees devoted to new products, customer service, strategic alliances, and other business functions. I asked for volunteers to serve on the major committees, and made sure that members from each department were present.

The committees used many of the ideas and worksheets in this book to monitor performance and progress toward our goal of 100 percent employee ownership. The worksheets allow for self-measurement. Employees become responsible for deciding what work needs to be done, and then for measuring what they do.

In 1996, Merritt Publishing became a 100 percent employee-owned company. This was not the end of the game—new challenges immediately confronted us, which meant, once again, a reevaluation of who we were and where we wanted to go. It meant a new business plan and a new game plan.

In 1998, we were approached with a new opportunity, and the employees voted unanimously to sell the company to a large computer-based training company. They believed in their abilities and wanted to participate as a player in the e-learning market. Many employees had ambitions to start and run their own companies where they would deal with the challenges and opportunities of growth and people management like we did as a group.

LIVING THE VISION

As a business leader, creating an overarching vision can have a profound effect on all aspects of your business. To do your job well, you have to start with four broad intentions:

1. To create the vision and mission that define your purpose.

2. To communicate these clearly and effectively and to translate the vision and mission into goals, objectives, and action items down to the individual level.

3. To measure success and encourage progress through others.

4. To stay the course and refocus on making changes in your action plan as needed.

If you accomplish these four goals, you've gone a long way toward realizing a fifth goal:

5. To build a culture that makes your company a good place to work—and thus improves your prospects for success. You need to give your company a strong sense of purpose.

If you achieve all of this, you'll truly be able to take control of your dreams. You'll be living your vision. Remember, the main goal is to avoid getting so busy managing today's business that tomorrow's business gets pushed aside. Goals are most useful when they help you decide what you and other employees should be doing at work today to help you achieve what you want for the future.

AN ONGOING PROCESS

When you've set the basic objectives you need to run a company efficiently, you'll usually find you've done much more work than you realized. These tools don't always come easily to entrepreneurial managers. You might doubt the value of something as abstract as a vision statement. But give the matter a chance—exercises that seem simplistic to you may have a fundamental impact on your employees or customers.

Think of your business as a place in which every person involved plays an indispensable role. This is an ongoing process that lasts as long as your company is in business. It's not over when your salespeople sign a customer. It's not over when you cash that customer's check. It's not over when you ship your product.

If ever, it's over when the phone rings again, and the same customer places another order. And then the whole process starts once more.

TOOLS FOR MOVING FROM VISION TO ACTION

In this chapter, we'll work through the following tasks within this ongoing process:

- Creating your vision.
- Crafting a mission statement.
- Doing the SWOT analysis.
- Defining corporate goals and objectives.
- Action plans: Turning vision into action.
- Visually representing your plan.

When you've finished, you should have a good idea of the best practical goals you can set for your company. You should be able to look toward the horizon without tripping over any obstacles at your feet.

Before we begin, ask yourself these questions about the future of your company:

- Have you spent time, no matter how long your business has existed, in thinking about the future of your business?
- Is your thinking about the future something you have adequately communicated to others who are involved in the business?
- Has your thinking about the future changed due to changes in the market, the economy, and technology?
- Are you willing to do whatever it takes to get to that future? Are you passionate and excited about the possibilities?

CREATING YOUR VISION

In a world where advances in automation and productivity have transformed many traditional value-added businesses into commodities, successful companies need a strong sense of purpose. The vision is a response to questions like: What does your company do? Why does it do that?

To have a purpose and communicate it passionately is the essence of leadership. The vision should be formulated by the founder, CEO, or chair of the board—the person who is responsible for the future of the business. This is the statement of your decision to act, and a definition for what direction that action will take. You cannot lead a group of people unless you set a direction.

A vision statement uses the future to help analyze the present. As the head of your operation, you have to articulate the blend of present and future. Expressing corporate purpose is the most important task management has.

A company needs a vision statement that everyone from the CEO to the receptionist can understand. It formulates what an organization wants to be and stimulates specific goals that can be passed down to every department in the organization. It needs to be something useful and applicable to daily operations. You—and, more importantly, your coworkers—should feel comfortable using your vision statement in everyday conversation.

Indeed, vision means something to people at all levels in an organization. All employees might not know the specifics of the company's marketing plans or financial outlook, but they do know its reputation. They know how other players in the industry or local market perceive it. They know when they work for a quality-driven organization, or one that's content to skim margins from second- or third-rate work.

If you build an environment that values quality, in which people can be proud of their efforts, you'll find better people more easily. And you'll be able to keep them once you've found them. But you can't achieve quality without explicitly saying you want to achieve it. It isn't something people infer from all companies. It isn't something you can effect passively. You have to set it up as a goal and pursue it continuously.

Something you'll find as you do this: People—employees, vendors, customers—want to believe in quality. Quality is rare enough that it has intrinsic value. People will work hard when they understand a vision that seeks quality performance. That kind of vision empowers people to perform well.

GREAT VISION

Sam Walton had a vision for Wal-Mart. He believed that giving a median to low-end retail customers in smaller geographic markets the widest possible choice of inexpensive goods would establish his chain as the market leader among discount department stores. His vision was this:

> To offer all the fine customers in our territories all of their household needs in a manner in which they continue to think of us fondly.

Ray Kroc's vision for McDonald's was that people could find fast, tasty food consistently wherever they traveled. One of the goals of McDonald's is that the food in all of its stores—all over the world—tastes exactly the same. And that its customers have a clean pleasant place to eat it. This is clear in reading the McDonald's vision statement:

> To be the world's best quick service restaurants experience. McDonald's accomplishes this by providing each customer with outstanding Quality, Service, Cleanliness and Value.

What is remarkable is that so many employees at all levels in both these organizations still share the founder's original vision.

Making It Happen

As you approach the task of defining your vision, first, spend some time talking with someone close to you about your company and your dreams for it: Ask yourself why you started your company, what you wanted to accomplish, the legacy you want to leave personally and professionally.

Your vision should have several elements: It must be long term, meaningful in a human context, and appeal to a higher purpose. A vision statement is not easy to write in a sentence or two, but writing it will make it clear to you and meaningful to others.

What do good vision statements have in common? You feel you know the company when you read them. They give the company a human feeling,

Results come when people develop a shared vision of how they want their organization to be perceived and are willing to work every day to maintain that vision.

a personality. They set out what the company values. They often refer to quality of life issues.

Try several drafts by answering these questions:

- What do you see your company becoming in 5 to 10 years?
- What values are an essential part of who you are and what you want your company to be?
- What innovations will your customers be looking for if they knew what was possible?

Reality Check

Circulate your vision statement drafts and edit and rewrite them until you feel good about them. Remember, the goal is for everyone in your company to believe in your vision; therefore, be sure to get the opinions of different people throughout the organization. Next, make sure it answers these questions:

- Who are you as a company?
- Where do you want to make your mark?
- How high do you want to shoot?
- What do you believe in?
- Does what you have written embody the spirit of where you want your company to head?
- Can you live with this vision? Are you willing to (or more appropriately, do you automatically) act in accordance with what you have written your vision to be?

If you find your new vision statement doesn't jive with the above questions, then don't be afraid to start anew. Defining your vision is an essential responsibility, and you might not get it right on the first few tries.

CRAFTING A MISSION STATEMENT

As you develop your overarching vision, you can use this process of self-exploration to determine your mission statement as well. These are two different entities—what the vision statement is to strategy, the mission statement is to tactics. It identifies the critical processes that impact implementation of vision. The vision statement will endure much longer than the mission statement. The vision statement will change only if the core purpose of the business changes. The mission statement may change as competition or technology changes.

You should have at least one mission statement for your company—and you may develop related ones for each distinct department or division. You may also want to develop temporary mission statements to communicate a current focus.

A good mission statement gets people to act in agreement with the company's broader goals. It reminds them how to behave every day, regardless of what temporary forces work against them, so that they can help realize the company's vision.

The mission of a company is not dreamy, like a vision. It is based in today and reality. It defines specifically your product and your market—who you will sell to and what you will sell.

A complete mission statement clearly and fully describes which factors—and, if necessary, which resources—are most critical to supporting the business strategy. The three factors that most managers consider in terms of their mission are:

1. *Quality* and reliability must be defined in terms of the customer (externally) and projected back (internally) to determine their impact on product development and operations. Internal quality benchmarks, as useful as they can be in monitoring operations, don't play as vital a role in developing a mission statement as do customer needs and wants. You have to consider the level and meaning of quality and reliability appropriate to the desired competitive position in the marketplace.

2. *Value* can mean lowest manufacturing cost, lowest selling price, or best quality for the money when other factors are considered. The first two definitions are fairly objective. Even though many management gurus stress so-called "best value," that definition tends to be so vague that it's useless.

3. *Service* includes more than just the friendliness of the greeting a customer hears when your receptionist picks up the phone. It translates into the degree to which you can devote company

resources to the needs of a specific customer—without ignoring all others. As we'll consider later, this has much to do with operations. Service entails manufacturing flexibility and versatility, the ability to produce a large variety of products of various volumes to supply a diverse market—and to do so quickly.

No organization can succeed by concentrating on any one of these factors to the exclusion of the other two. Your challenge is to balance the resources you apply to each in proportion to priorities based on current situations and future positions.

Management should agree on functional mission statements that identify the operating resources that are critical to support the business strategy. For example, Domino's Pizza made a dramatic change in emphasis when it changed its mission statement. Domino's was known in the pizza delivery business for its 30-minute delivery guarantee. It discontinued its 30-minute guarantee in 1993 and replaced it with this simple statement:

Exceptional people on a mission to be the best pizza delivery company in the world.

In those few words, Domino's shifted its corporate emphasis from speed to quality.

While a mission statement can be as simple as defining the product and the market, some companies feel that the way they treat employees and customers is just as important in defining who they are as is the product and market. For example, since the late 1980s, the big players in the U.S. automobile industry have focused mission statements on reducing new product realization (the time passing from concept to the cars in the showroom) from 48 months to the 12 months that carmakers like Honda can boast. Ford, General Motors, and Chrysler have all raised their quality standards to match their foreign competitors, but they suffer in comparison because they take so long to respond to market demands.

General Motors decided to create a new paradigm with Saturn. Its mission statement is intended to benefit not just customers but the whole organization of which it is a part:

[Our goal is to] market vehicles developed and manufactured in the United States that are world leaders in quality, cost, and customer satisfaction through the integration of people, technology, and business system and to transfer knowledge, technology, and experience throughout General Motors.

As Saturn's many devoted customers can attest, this is a different kind of company within the GM conglomerate, and its mission statement sets the tone with its customer-oriented practices.

Making It Happen

The discussion that can lead to preparing this portion of the mission statement may be the most important part of creating it. To be able to clearly define your market may be a more difficult task than you would think.

Look at your own promotional catalogs to see if all of your products have a similar theme that you can define. Like Federal Express, is your primary product speed? Like Nordstrom, is your primary product quality in terms of service? Or like Apple computer, is your primary product quality in terms of ease of installation and use? Like Wal-Mart, is your primary product wide selection?

Get a list of your customers and look for their similarities. Is your market who you thought they would be? Can everyone who buys from you be classified as a particular group? Or like FedEx, is your market almost everyone?

Take these preliminary ideas to your employees and see if they agree. Have meetings just to discuss these items. Then test them in the outside world. Draft your mission statement from these questions:

- What do you sell?

- To whom do you sell it?

- What does your company do better or want to do better than anyone else?

- How does your company rank the importance of quality, value, and service?

- How do you define each of these based on customer needs and expectations?

- How will you achieve your vision?

Reality Check

As with the vision statement, circulate your drafts and edit and rewrite them until you feel good about them. Then ask yourself and others these questions:

- Does your mission statement capture what makes you unique as a company?

- Would your customers and vendors recognize you in these statements? Would they be pleasantly surprised because they could really buy in to these directions?

- Are they directions your customers would agree with?

- Is your mission statement inspiring?

- Does this give everyone in your company direction for each day when they walk in the door? Is there any ambiguity in what is most important?

- If an employee faced a difficult dilemma at work, would thinking of your mission statement lead them to make the right decision?

ANALYZING YOUR STRENGTHS, WEAKNESSES, OPPORTUNITIES, AND THREATS

To begin to make certain that the vision and mission are attainable, many companies participate in an exercise called a *SWOT Analysis.* SWOT stands for Strengths, Weaknesses, Opportunities, and Threats. The system stresses a more complete perspective on what accounts for success in a company. It was originally developed by the Massachusetts-based Boston Consulting Group in the early 1970s.

The SWOT Analysis works well because it contrasts the internal and external factors that affect a company. It matches the strengths found in the company's internal environment with opportunities in the organization's external environment in a way that makes its core competencies self-evident.

Scanning the internal environment includes an analysis of the company's structure, its culture, and its resources. Here are just some of the areas that should be considered in SWOT Analysis:

Strengths. Our strengths are our core competencies—those things we do better than any of our competitors or that really tie together all the products we offer in a unique way. What internal structures or expertise do we have that are a special source of pride? This becomes the center for determining what we will do in the future. We want to constantly build on the things we already do particularly well.

Weaknesses. For every thing we visualize clearly or do well, there is something we can't see so clearly or do so well. Some of these weaknesses we can change—others we can't. Where do we need to build our company? What is holding us back or creating a bottleneck for everyone else? If we choose to spend money or other resources in one direction, in what other directions might we be tolerating or creating weaknesses?

Ask yourself whether the following things are strengths or weaknesses for your company:

- Product quality.
- Quality of the management staff.
- Quality of technical staff.
- Brand name.
- Planning process.
- Quality of staff performance management system.
- Profitability.
- Availability of cash for growth.
- Quality of marketing and sales efforts.
- Compliance with legal requirements.
- Facilities.
- Operations.
- Staff morale.

The Opportunities/Threats portion of the SWOT looks at factors outside of your company, but which will have a profound affect on your ultimate success. Scanning the external environment clarifies your future opportunities, but also forces a company to face problems that could threaten the company's survival if not taken into account.

Opportunities. The most difficult thing about opportunity is recognizing it. The old adage about opportunity knocking once does apply in many cases, so we need to see it—and be able to act on it—when it comes. What are our greatest challenges in the changing environment of the industries we serve? How will new technologies help us? What will our customers need in the future that we can supply? What opportunities will open up globally?

Threats. As with weaknesses, there are some threats we can minimize and there are others we can't. We need to do all we can to control the threats we can predict—and prepare for the ones we can't. What outside our control could threaten our existence? How might new technology hurt us? What in the political environment (government) might threaten us? Will ups or downs in the economy hurt us? What in our physical environment might threaten us? Remember to consider the following factors:

- Market limitations.
- Lack of availability of capital.
- Problems with suppliers.
- Natural disasters.
- Location challenges.
- Quality of labor pool.
- Revolutionary changes in the industry.
- Governmental regulations.
- Technological changes.
- Socio-political challenges.

Making It Happen

The point is to build on your strengths, limit your weaknesses, capitalize on your opportunities, and survive the threats to your business. Devising a strategy for doing each is key.

This is a tool often used for a group discussion by key people and for good feedback to management of how employees view the company. A SWOT Analysis can be done for the company as a whole, as well as for various departments. This is how I use the process:

- Divide a blank sheet of paper into quadrants, marking a heading for each of Strengths, Weaknesses, Opportunities, and Threats.

- Give copies to key staff members and ask them for their analysis independently. Then ask for all the input brought in from each member of the group in each of the four categories.

- Write out all ideas on a board in front of the group, and then pick 7 to 10 of the items in each category that seem best to fit your company. As with many management issues, the challenge for you is to judge well which items under each heading are key and which aren't.

When you've identified Strengths, Weaknesses, Opportunities, and Threats, you can compare each to your vision and mission statements.

Reality Check

Doing the list is just the first step. Now look at your list and ask yourself these questions:

- Are you using your strengths to their fullest capacity? Are they things you could leverage by teaching them to more people to develop more product, market better, or be more efficient?

- Do your weaknesses and threats make your vision and mission unrealistic? If there are illogical connections or inconsistencies, what do they mean?

- Do you celebrate what you do well enough?

- Why have you chosen to live with your weaknesses? Would eliminating these be painful? Result in difficult staff changes or cultural changes? Are they financially costly to resolve?

- What is holding you back from taking advantage of your opportunities?

- Are your competitors taking better advantage of these than you are?

- What can *you* do immediately to minimize threats?

- Do you have plans to minimize the damage if any of these threats become a reality?

DEFINING CORPORATE GOALS

The next step in the process of analyzing your company and defining your vision is to set your corporate goals and objectives.

Corporate objectives turn vision and mission into specific items to be accomplished. They should also be written to include specific measurements to know if success has been achieved.

Corporate goals can be set for many years in advance. With the current pace of change, focus on three years out at the most for setting real objectives. Objectives must be updated often and most companies set a planning structure to update them on an annual basis. You want to do the most detailed planning for work you decide is the next step toward your vision—work that can and should be done right away or in the next 12 months.

Corporate objectives must be set at the corporate level. They should be big, bold, and highly motivational. But there shouldn't be too many of them or they dilute the possibility of accomplishing any. Two is probably too few, nine too many—five always seems like a good number to me.

The corporate objectives should also be realistic. The goal for a small dry cleaning establishment to grow to $10 million in revenue its first year is not going to be good for the owner or the employees. A more realistic growth plan, perhaps to open four new stores in the next three years, will make a better goal.

Ultimately, there should be subobjectives set for all aspects of the business. You should set goals for constant improvement in all segments of the business, even if you focus more of your time, attention, and resources in certain areas. You may never set a corporate goal to streamline your accounting department, but that might be a subobjective to an overall cost-cutting strategy.

Good measures will have numbers and times attached to them. Here are some examples of goals and objectives:

- We will have 20 new customers at the end of the year.
- We will have a 10 percent market share in our main product line.
- Our substantial investment in R&D will allow us to have three new products in the pipeline in 18 months.
- We will generate gross revenues of $1 million per quarter.
- Our gross profit margin will increase from 28 percent to 33 percent by the end of the coming quarter due to cost-cutting initiatives.
- We will open three new locations over the next 12 months.
- We will increase our workforce to 70 employees by the end of the quarter.
- The business will have a net worth of $14 million in 5 years.
- I intend to sell the business in 3 years, so it must have a competent management team in place by the end of year 2.

Making It Happen

Although corporate objectives are set by leaders and managers, they may begin as a negotiation between the owner or CEO and the managers of the company. The owners or the board want certain things accomplished this year. The managers don't know if those things are doable given what they know about the capabilities of the company. The discussion of whether the profit goal of 10 percent is realistic this year is important.

The owner or CEO should decide corporate objectives based on what trends have led to this point, what resources are available to the organization this

Once you decide what to do, you have to decide who does the work—and this takes you to the action plan. Here you break down the work by department, team, and individual. You let each one know what part it plays in the overall plan, when it must complete a given task, and how it can measure its own success.

year, and what opportunities are open in the market. The objectives chosen should be explained in detail to managers with a focus on why they are right for the company at this time.

At a separate meeting, managers should have the opportunity to counter the selected objectives or validate them. Why don't managers think they are achievable? What would it take in terms of additional resources to make them achievable? Is the CEO willing to provide those resources?

While the owner or CEO must make the final decision about the annual objectives, it should only be after lively debate with key managers and others. It is more likely that the achievements will be met if people agree with them or at least have an understanding of their formulation.

Reality Check

Corporate objectives must be meaningful to the people responsible for accomplishing them. Ask yourself these questions to see if your objectives are realistic:

- Do your objectives further the intent of your vision and mission?
- If you completed all of the objectives, would you feel you have accomplished something that is key for the company's overall success?
- Are the objectives realistic within the time frame allotted?
- Are the objectives realistic, given the circumstances of the current market?
- Are the objectives realistic, given your resources in terms of staff ability, time, and money?

ACTION PLANS: TURNING VISION INTO ACTION

Once you have determined your vision, mission, and corporate objectives, you must then set into motion more specific plans of action. This includes defining the person responsible for different aspects of the plan and assigning specific due dates.

Action plans are marching orders and provide very specific directions.

This is the essence of employee participation in the planning process. Some people enjoy the freedom of a blank piece of paper to dream about what they would like to accomplish. Most, however, just want to know that they can make a contribution.

Try to make it clear exactly what you—and your managers—want this exercise to accomplish. Done well, these action plans can become milestones that you use to gauge performance and progress. That goes for individuals, departments, and the company as a whole.

In many cases, this is an appropriate part of a person's annual performance and compensation review. In other cases, you use them on a project-specific basis. Because action plans are so straightforward, they're useful in almost any managerial context.

Making It Happen

Give each person who works with you all of the material developed so far (vision, mission, and corporate objectives) and then encourage each to write his or her own action plans, linking them to specific corporate objectives.

These action items should be discussed with the manager who sets the objectives. They can become part of the employee's personal goals for the year, and compensation decisions can be made using accomplishment of these specific goals as part of the decision process.

There are also objectives within a department or involving more than one department that can only be met with a team of people. Pick the team of people, or ask for volunteers, and give them the appropriate worksheet to use to develop action items as a group.

Some individuals are much more creative verbally than in writing. Encourage people to sit down with peers from other departments to talk through the meaning of each objective and how their individual work can help contribute. Notes taken from these discussions can translate into meaningful action items.

If *you* establish this process as a credible exercise, your people will tell you things you might not have thought of before. And if you can tie a person's paycheck into what you want them to accomplish, and also make sure they are recognized for their achievements by their peers, you can almost be certain that they will meet the objectives that they themselves set.

Once action items are set, negotiate deadlines for completion. Before they are finally written, deadlines should be agreed on between the manager and the employee, and interim deadlines should be set if there are long or complex projects.

Reality Check

Ask each person who is responsible for the action items to help you and others determine if the action items are appropriate for them. Have them answer these questions:

- Do these action items work toward meeting the objective set?

- If all the action items under a single objective are met, will the objective be met?

- Are these action items clear enough to give employees adequate direction?

- Is there any ambiguity about what successful accomplishment means?

- Is the employee/group committed to getting these things done?

- Does the employee/group think these plans are realistic considering the current workload?

- Are there adequate resources available to make these action plans possible?

VISUALLY REPRESENTING YOUR PLAN

Frontline workers often complain that they're not told where and how their efforts fit into the company as a whole. That feeling can be a major disincentive to effective work and innovation. Take every chance you can to help your coworkers understand that their contributions make a difference to the company.

It is vital to take the vision/mission, corporate objectives, and action plans out of your head and develop them visually as a communications tool. You must translate into graphic form the concepts, objectives, and goals you've set out in other exercises.

Pulling together all of the elements from this chapter, we can visually show how each section draws from the previous to make up our game plan. It compares different exercises in relation to one another and their overall importance in the management process. This is a powerful tool for communicating all of the pieces of the planning cycle to your people and for letting them see where their work fits into the whole.

Making It Happen

Colorful eye-catching visual communication is inspiring and exciting. When I was CEO of a publishing company, we tried to be as creative as we could when we used graphics to represent important business concepts. We tried a number of different methods, from using glass jars and beads to toy horses on a track to stacks of books.

A graphic can compare statistics or trends that don't always leap to mind as relevant but, together, shed insight and understanding on a key business function. This kind of graphic tells everyone where he or she fits in the planning process—usually something companies, especially big ones, keep trapped in the boardroom.

One of the methods we liked best was to create a wall-size circle and post it in a common area. In the center, we put the company vision. In the next concentric circle out, we placed the mission. This was followed by the corporate objectives. Ultimately, each department and then each individual was named with his or her own action items. This showed a direct link between the company's vision and the individual's course of action. Keeping several years of these circles in a conference room reminded us of how much we had accomplished.

Use your imagination to add color and graphics as appropriate to communicate your direction to everyone, every day. Encourage people to study the visual representation—and even have employees and managers cross off items that have been completed, and date them at companywide meetings. Celebrate each of these significant events. If you can develop a graphic that lives on the computer, it can be changed in real time and made available to all employees when they wish to see it.

Reality Check

Looking at your visual representation of your vision, mission, objectives, and action items, consider these questions:

- Do you have a sense of a team pulling in one direction? Do any of the items you see contradict each other?

- Does this look like a year's worth of work? Are all of the items significant and meaningful?

- Are you excited by the work this represents? Does this visual help you imagine how you will feel when projects are completed?

- Is this document posted in a place where people will find themselves and mentally review their progress (and that of their peers) every day?

WHAT'S NEXT

In this chapter, we've started our work on a vision for the company and translating that vision into action. We are still in the planning stage. We take that planning stage closer to reality in the next chapter on budgeting. Budgeting is planning with dollars and it is through the budgeting process that we begin to know whether our vision can be translated into a profitable company.

PART II

SET HIGH STANDARDS

2

CREATING A BUDGET EVERYONE CAN USE AND UNDERSTAND

If you can't pay for a thing, don't buy it. If you can't get paid for it, don't sell it.

—*Benjamin Franklin*

One of the most grueling parts of running a small business is budgeting. Many people hate budgets; some to the point that they run their businesses using their daily bank balances as their only financial tool.

You, too, might resist the notion that you can benefit from good budgeting—until you try it. You would learn that budgeting takes some of the hazard out of business by minimizing the guesswork. Budgeting gives you a blueprint for action. It tells you what to expect and alerts you to trouble when the unexpected happens. Indeed, it is crucial to know how your business will accomplish the goals you set for it, and your budget measures your success; when your business outperforms your projections, you know you're doing well.

To benchmark your success, you can calculate certain financial and operating ratios that look at both your income statement and balance sheet, giving you an indication of your financial health over time. You will also want to compare your numbers against your competitors' and the industry standard. For most industries, it is possible to compare your ratios to the industry standard to get a sense of how financially competitive you are as a business. You will certainly want to strive to be in the top half, or better yet, the top quarter.

In this chapter, I take you through the basics of budgeting, showing how to put together a *bottom-up* budget—that is, an overall budget that reflects the real needs of your business. I present case studies that show the value of budgeting to a young business and to the business facing a crisis. I also include a number of worksheets at the end of this chapter to show you how to analyze your average selling prices, month-to-month unit sales, sales projections, payroll, expenses, and overall performance. First, I explain in more detail why the budget is so crucial and how to keep your budget under control in even the most volatile industries.

THE BUDGET SETS PRIORITIES

You send a direct message about the priorities of the company with what you spend your money on, as opposed to what you say with your vision or mission statement. You might say your company is committed to customer service, but if you spend little money training or staffing your customer hotlines and a great deal on your corporate facility, employees will know what your real commitment is.

PARTICIPATIVE BUDGETING

It's an oddity of traditional businesses that budgets come down from on high, from senior management, particularly from the finance department. The best budgets show the input of the people making the expenditures and focus on each business function in the company from the bottom up and starting with zero in each column of numbers. The best budgets reflect the thinking of the people who know best where the company really spends its money. Get the input of these people when you put your budgets and projections together.

Senior managers must also understand and have input into the numbers in the budget. Good budgeting is a highly interactive process. Whereas people may not argue for changes to the mission statement, they will almost certainly argue for changes in allowable spending. Budgets should be drafted, compared to the previous year's actual expenditures, debated for the best use of resources, and redrafted as necessary.

You should prepare budgets *after* you set direction with your vision and mission statements and corporate objectives. The budget is the next step in taking you from the generalities of your business plan to the specifics of day-to-day operations.

By setting priorities, the budget makes clear what your finances permit you to do to reach your goals. It translates the vision and mission statements and corporate objectives into action.

Above all, the budget is a tool for all people who have responsibility for spending money and making money, not just CEOs. The financial statements you show your directors, investors, and lenders don't tell managers what you expect from them and which of their efforts you value most; your budget does.

KNOW WHEN TO STOP

It is important to spend time creating your budget, but when you finish it, get back to daily business. The most important point is to have something to measure reality against, not to make the budget perfect. Budgeting becomes more realistic as time goes on. Budget 12 months in advance, and, if possible, update quarter by quarter to create a rolling 12-month budget. This enables you to make changes frequently enough to do reasonably accurate budgeting. Don't think too much about the budgeting process in the meantime.

In addition, build some tolerance for variance into your numbers. Your budget stops being accurate the moment you finish it, and when variances occur—and they will—make sure the numbers allow opportunity for your managers to act creatively. Although budgets should be designed to create accountability, accountability should be related to the real issues behind the numbers, not the numbers alone.

Remember that finance plays both operational and analytic roles. Some business owners become excessively enamored of quantitative analysis—to the detriment of qualitative analysis, which can lead to problems. When an overzealous finance department detects a companywide difficulty, it can make matters worse by forcing its priorities on other units rather than looking at the underlying problem.

One Illinois-based consultant offers a good example. When an internal audit finds too many assets tied up in inventory, he says, "out goes a memo telling all unit managers to cut inventory 25 percent in six months. Only the hot items move out fast. The rest sit there. When it's all over, inventories are down 10 percent, the CFO declares victory—and the only items left are the ones nobody wants."

PLAN FOR DEBT

Knowing where you stand can yield big benefits, as Andrea Totten discovered in running her California-based quilt-making company, Rags to Riches. She founded the company in 1971, selling quilts and comforters at flea markets and art fairs, then used a small catalog to generate orders from stores and designers. "[Business] started getting really busy and that's when I decided that I needed to find a direction," she says. "I guess then I didn't think of the word business plan, but I guess now in retrospect that's what it was."

Totten wrote proposals and went to a variety of lenders, only to find most reluctant to lend to small businesses and some, it seemed, reluctant to lend to women. "Even though I had a house and a car, they wouldn't take them [as collateral]," she says. "Each year they'd say, 'Come back in a year.' Meanwhile, four or five years passed."

Totten resorted to "asset based lending"—high-interest loans made against accounts receivable by fashion industry lenders called *factors*. "You sell your receivables," Totten says. "[The loans] were good at the time because they were needed. But they turned out to be too expensive to maintain."

The factors charged 4.5 percent interest per month. "The only way to beat it is to keep the money going. So once the business slows down, it's a killer," she says.

She persuaded a bank to lend her working capital when her billings passed half a million dollars. Still, Totten found herself devoting 20 percent of her cash flow to servicing debt. In addition, she didn't think her bankers valued small-company business; among other things, they frequently changed the terms of her credit line. She paid her loans down as quickly as she could and eventually got out of debt.

"By the time I took classes on how to write [business plans, the instructors assumed that] you sell $20,000 and the next month you have $20,000 in because the people always pay on time. Not true. Receivables don't come in that smoothly, and vendors want money. Your labor, of course, is COD," she says. "I brought in $80,000 in cash, where was it? The business plan was hard to keep to because of the fluctuations of our industry."

In the late 1980s, a number of Totten's competitors went out of business. Trouble plagued the retail industry, too. Stores that had always paid their bills on time now stalled her, stretching her receivables to $10,000 or $15,000 per store. Then suddenly they'd be gone, leaving her with lots of bad debt.

All this led Totten to manage her receivables strictly. "I never let anybody get high enough to ruin me if I lose," she says. "It's kind of like gambling. Don't ever gamble more than you can afford to lose. I look at my receivables and [decide which] people I'll put on COD. If they don't want to buy from me anymore, that's okay because I'm losing money [with them] anyway."

FOLLOW THE MONEY

Totten developed a number of strategies for staying on budget in a tumultuous industry. First, she downsized by attrition—that is, she opted not to replace employees who left. Once she had little or no short-term debt to preoccupy her, she could reassess her market, too. "I said: 'What do I want to do? Do I want to go and look for new business or do I want to better serve the business I have?' And I chose to stay with the stores that were loyal to me and not advertise."

In addition, Totten was selling to almost 1,000 retailers throughout the country. Whereas many entrepreneurs would look to add even more retailers, Totten felt that she was stretching herself too thin. She looked at the big customers who paid most reliably and cut back on doing business with the rest. In the end, she trimmed her customer list by two-thirds but maintained almost the same revenue. As she explains, "To me, there are two ways to go out of business. One is to have too many orders and the other is to have too few. I used to look at gross sales, but my accountant showed me if I sell $900,000 a year and my profits are higher, that's a success, not if I sell a million a year and my profits are down."

Totten also released her outside sales reps. They took 10 percent commissions and often didn't service the customer well, giving out the wrong information or not knowing the answers to key questions. "I [used to pay] two people to do the same job. Now we have our [in-house] reps call and customers fax the orders in. We call back and go over the order with them," she says.

Throughout this restructuring, she kept prices steady, protecting her margins. Her strategy translated into stiff terms with her customers. Rags to Riches doesn't give retailers discounts beyond those in its price list—and those only to retailers who display the company's wares prominently. "It's one thing to get into a new store, but its another thing to get re-orders," she says. In fact, she uses reorder trends as her main diagnostic test for how the company is doing. "If we don't get reorders, then we know that something's wrong. Either the salespeople don't know how to sell [the product] or it's not displayed correctly or it's in the wrong store."

Her final observation about taking control of her company's finances was that "Small business people have to keep up with what is happening just as much as a CEO at a huge corporation. If you're not on top of your finances on a real-time basis you're not going to make it." Thirty plus years later, Rags to Riches produces bedding and upholstered furniture along with hand-painted furniture in a 13,000-square foot facility and employs a staff of 50.

CONTROL EXPENSES

Andrea Totten grew her business by remaining flexible and by keeping an attentive eye on her market. She controlled expenses and reshaped her finances to fit her needs. She learned the value of understanding the impact of finances on her business.

Totten's example holds some valuable lessons, including these:

- *Evaluate your projections regularly,* particularly when adding capital to your business (whether yours or somebody else's).

- *If you have a hunch about the future, follow it*—but look for similar surprises in the past and find out what impact they had. Don't simply adjust your financial projections on instinct. Instead, base your new thinking on as much hard evidence as you can gather. Your hunch may tell you that an upturn lies around the corner—but that new market you pursue may trail the overall economy by a year.

The owners of new businesses often review every expense, but as things progress, they back off. They control expenses with budgets and paper trails—that is, invoices and purchase orders—and make sure that only a few, accountable people handle cash.

Once your business is established, you should spend most of your budgeting time on the big numbers, where most of your money is spent. The major categories are revenue, payroll, inventory costs, marketing and sales, facility, insurance, computers, and others that may be related to your particular business. Here are some simple reminders about holding down expenses:

- *Purchasing.* In a small business, put one person—not five or six—in charge of ordering merchandise and using overnight mail services.

- *Supplies.* Make your employees aware of the costs of office supplies; some managers mark the individual cost of each item, such as pens, on the box. Hold your managers responsible for expenses in their departments. Keep an eye out for hard-to-budget costs such as delivery fees. You may spend less to send an hourly worker to pick up supplies.

- *Travel and entertainment.* Scrutinize expenses such as travel and entertainment. Trips should be planned in advance when possible to take advantage of travel discounts, especially some of those now found on the Internet. Make sure that travel and entertainment expenses pay off with increased business.

- *Professional fees.* Negotiate fees paid to lawyers, accountants, and consultants by the project or the period of time, or even their hourly rate. Set caps on what can be spent without specific approval.

- *Computers and related costs.* A great deal of money has been spent in the past few years on personal computers and software, most of it necessary. Set a budget for computer hardware and a separate budget for software and technical support.

PLAN FOR CASH

Unfortunately, in most businesses, cash coming in lags behind cash going out. For instance, you may have to pay for inventory or raw materials months before you receive money on the products they produced. This requires cash flow planning. Your budget may be right, but it may not take into consideration when the cash has to go out and when it will come in. Many businesses use a line of credit to plan for this lag time.

Get a line of credit when your business is doing well—when you don't need it. When you do need it, you probably won't qualify to get it.

Knowing how to slow down spending and collect what others owe you are skills essential in any business. These skills give you access to the cash you need to grow or to stay in the game.

Accounts payable are the bills from vendors. It is often possible to negotiate terms that will allow you to hold on to your money longer. For instance, you may be able to pay bills in 45 days instead of the customary 30 (this varies by industry) if you make arrangements beforehand.

When a company is facing a financial downturn, one of the first things it does is slow down the paying of its bills. It may be unable to borrow from a bank at that point, so it borrows from its vendors. It is important to know how to do this well, as well as to know when it is being done to you. If you find you need to pay bills late, the most important thing is to maintain communications with your vendors. It would be expensive for them to have to forcibly collect these monies from you, so they will likely be willing to hang in there for some time, as long as you provide them with a plan for repayment. This is particularly important if you need to keep purchasing from them during your financial crisis.

Do not get in the habit of paying your vendors late unless necessary. When it becomes necessary, you will need the track record of a good payment history to convince them to give you extra time. Especially in tight industry niches, word travels about who pays on time and who doesn't. The day may come when you need a favor from a vendor who feels ill-used or when a credit agency downgrades your payment rating.

Accounts receivable are monies that your customers owe you for product already delivered. The object is to collect this money as quickly as possible. Coming from the opposite perspective, it is important to know the top (at least) 10 customers who owe you money and to track their payment habits. You are more likely to be paid if you keep in regular communication with them and they need your services on an ongoing basis. You should specify a maximum amount of credit you are willing to extend to each customer, and watch carefully any customers at the upper end of that limit. Don't loan more than you can afford to lose.

BUDGET FOR THE BIG ITEMS

Another kind of budgeting that companies must do is budgeting for the big-ticket items that can be depreciated over time. *Depreciation* allows you to take the expense of the big item into your records over time so that you have a more even profit picture year to year. Real estate, a building, a computer system, or other large equipment are examples of these big-ticket items, called *capital expenditures*. You should budget for these expenditures separately because they don't go into your income statement. *Income statements* are intended to represent your revenue and expenses from regular operations, not extraordinary one-time purchases.

PLAN FOR PROFITS

Even if cash lags behind, always plan to make a profit. You may be able to get through short periods where your expenses are higher than your revenue, especially when you first start in business, but it will catch up with you. However, in spite of your careful budgeting, the truth is that revenue is often less than expected, and expenses are usually more than expected. Knowing this, budget enough of an excess to allow for a margin of error to ensure a reasonable profit.

What makes for a reasonable profit varies by business, industry, and is usually affected by the economy as well. Some years, survival itself is a victory. In other years, building up a cash reserve to protect yourself in the down years (and expect that there will be some if you are in business long enough) is essential.

For the long run, it is essential to develop a business that prospers in both an up and down economy—preferably with some products or services that sell well when the economy is great and others that people need when times are tough.

SET FINANCIAL CONTROLS

Budgeting and sharing financial information with employees doesn't mean loosening the reins on financial controls and checks and balances to prevent errors and theft. It is estimated that employee theft may cause U.S. businesses as much as $100 billion each year. Discuss with your CPA the best methods you can use to prevent fraud and embezzlement. I found the following essential both for my own peace of mind and the protection of my employees:

SIX THINGS YOU CAN DO TO PREVENT EMPLOYEE FRAUD

1. Mail should be opened immediately, and checks received should be individually recorded by someone other than the bookkeeper.

2. Checks should be stamped "For Deposit Only" and deposited the same day received.

3. Purchase orders or other documentation must be required for every check written. Approval requirements should be set depending on the size of the check.

4. Bank statements must be reconciled monthly by someone outside the accounting department. At one time, I had statements sent to my home instead of to the office.

5. The same person should not be buying inventory and receiving inventory.

6. It is always a red flag if accounting or purchasing employees never take vacations. They can't afford to have someone else examine their files for a week or two because it might be discovered that they have been stealing from the company.

In summary, budgets serve as defensive mechanisms against risk, alerting the organization to problems lying ahead by building on the past. The important thing is to stay in the game. If you have losses and let those losses continue, you will eventually run out of cash. It usually happens slowly—you have a line of credit that you have maxed out or can't pay back. You take longer and longer to pay your bills. You spend a greater percentage of your time stalling creditors and looking for any source of cash. Eventually, if this continues, you come up to a payday with too little cash to meet payroll. That may be your last day in business. However, budgeting lets you know in advance that you may have a shortfall. If you budget, you will have plenty of opportunity to make changes in your operations to avoid that situation altogether.

In addition, successful companies use their budgeting to identify specific, realistic, and quantifiable goals. Budgets bring order to the task of pursuing those goals. First, you identify a revenue or sales objective for the year. Then, identify the tasks necessary to reach that objective. That done, explore the costs and budget for them, outlining the time and resources you must commit to reach the goal. The budget quantifies your plan in dollars. It also tells your managers and employees what you value as an owner or manager.

Remember that you don't win when bankers or customers allow you to use their money. You win when you pay them off. For new businesses, the first order of business is to pay off lenders. Particularly when you consider that owners of new businesses generally sign personal guarantees for bank loans, leases, and company credit cards, and in some cases with their biggest suppliers in order to get the best credit terms. The quickest way to get to financial stability is to identify basic financial factors and measure them, so that you can make midcourse corrections. Here are some final tips for successful budgeting:

- Don't keep your budgets and financial projections in a drawer. Use them to chart the implementation of your strategies. There's no guarantee that careful budgeting and financial analysis will bring the success you want, but without them, failure becomes more likely.

- Scrutinize every potential risk that your business faces. That means looking at—and sometimes looking beyond—the bottom line.

REVENUE FORECASTS

Now that we've covered the importance of a realistic budget and how to control your budget, we turn to calculating your budget. The two components to the budget, which are done separately and then put together, are revenue (sales) and expenses (costs). Generally, you will do the revenue budget first, using the sales unit quantity numbers as a base for both the sales dollars and expenses.

Revenue forecasts are much more difficult to determine with accuracy than expense budgets. You might be successful forecasting an increase in revenue as 20 percent from the prior year, but you lose the importance of the process. Instead, look at trends in your business and outside your business and take a hard look at what will be different this year. Do you forecast a 20 percent increase in sales this year just because you think it will look better if you do or because of a new product, an increasing market, or an upswing in the economy? In addition, if possible, you should base your revenue dollars forecast on expected units to be sold—number of customers, transactions, renewal sales, products produced, and type of product.

The easiest way to begin a projection is to map out at least one year—but no more than three years—based on your performance over the same period in the past. If you don't have that much history, start with the projections you made in your business plan, adjusted to actual performance since you opened for business.

Put *expenses* into categories (examples follow later in the chapter) that make sense in your business. The most important thing is to define what expenses you want in each of these categories so that you have some consistency for comparing actual with budget and can accurately trend the numbers over time.

Budget according to what actual expenses have been in the past, but be proactive as well. Determine a reasonable amount to spend on office supplies and budget accordingly. You can establish other benchmarks by comparing your expenses with other companies in your industry. If you belong to a trade group, find out how other members have done relative to their projections. Have they come in over or under their projections? Did they miss or exceed the mark by less than 5 percent—or by more than 10? Try to find out how specific competitors have done. If all else fails, find out how businesses in your region do in general.

PROFITS DETERMINE SURVIVAL

Profits aren't everything in business; in fact, your vision statement probably says nothing about profits. However, without profits and their conversion to cash, no business survives long enough to reach its goals. Fittingly, therefore, almost everything in budgeting stems from the simple formula for determining profit: revenue minus expenses. This formula drives business. Profit ultimately defines performance, in other words. Everything else is elaboration.

TOOLS FOR CREATING A BUDGET EVERYONE CAN USE

The following exercises will help you to create a bottom-up budget:

- Revenue budgeting.

- Expense budgeting.

- Budget notebook.

- Payroll projections.

- Income statement projections.

- Balance sheet projections.

- Break-even analysis.

REVENUE BUDGET

Revenue budgeting is a series of steps to determine how much you are selling, in terms of units; how much each unit is bringing in, in terms of dollars; and when to expect the dollars, in terms of time.

The four worksheets in this section are:

1. Average selling price per product.

2. Unit sales by product.

3. Dollar sales projections by product.

4. Dollar sales projections by month.

Even if your business is a service business rather than a product business, you can do a modified form of this analysis. You can count by number of customers instead of units of products.

AVERAGE SELLING PRICE PER PRODUCT

To begin to project your sales for the year, it is essential to know how much you are selling of each unit of product now. Worksheet 2.1 considers pricing issues across all product lines in detail. This is critical if you discount your prices for volume or other criteria. You may think your prices are close to retail, but the average price may be at a deeper discount than you think.

This worksheet is useful in making pricing decisions. Some industries have standard discounts and pricing schedules required by retailers from wholesalers.

If you know you must make at least $10 per unit to be profitable and the discount required by retailers is 50 percent, you must set your retail price at $20 minimum.

The trend in average price per product may also give some important signs about your business and your industry. If the average selling price drops consistently from year to year (as, for example, with computer software), you will have to become much more efficient in production to remain profitable.

Worksheet 2.1 also gives you valuable information about what your customers are willing to pay for your products. After calculating the average selling price per product, compare this to what your largest customers are paying. Are they buying far below this number? Are some of your larger customers willing to buy at a number higher than this?

This approach to determining price per unit may be too basic for companies with complex product lines (though the theory behind price per unit measurement remains useful). It will work in many cases.

Making It Happen

To calculate average price per product, list your products in column A and their total sales volume in column B of Worksheet 2.1. In column C, list how many units were sold of each. In column D, list the selling price for each unit of the product. To compute the average price per unit in column E, divide column B by column C. For F, the average discount from

Worksheet 2.1
Average Selling Price per Product

☐ This past year
☐ Two years ago

A Product	B Total $ Sales	C # of Units Sold	D Selling Price $ per Unit	E Average Price $ per Unit (B/C)	F % of Selling Price (E/D)

the selling price, divide column E by column D. Complete this exercise for at least two years' worth of information.

Reality Check

Consider these questions about your completed worksheet:

- Has your average price per unit decreased or increased over the past two years?

- How have your selling prices increased or decreased over the same period of time?

- Are discounts—as a percentage—about the same over the past two years or have they stayed the same? Do you have to give up a larger percentage of total revenues over time?

- Is one customer large enough to be responsible for a sizable drop in average price per product? Can your discounting policy be changed to encourage purchase of higher margin?

UNIT SALES BY PRODUCT

It is important to begin any series of sales projections with what your actual unit sales were the previous year. Sales dollars may be increasing year to year because of price increases, while unit volume may actually be decreasing.

The number of things that you sell—regardless of price or terms—reflects the underlying strength of your business. If unit sales aren't increasing, you aren't growing in real terms.

Keep the actual numbers that come from these worksheets over time. All products have life cycles. You will see which products have consistent sales and which have increasing or decreasing sales. Generally, a handful of products have unit sales much greater than expected (although dollar sales might be right on target or even below expectations). Most have sales slightly below our usually optimistic projections.

Unit sales are a much better method of measuring real growth than are dollar sales. *Dollar sales* can be impacted by price changes, additional charges, and so on. Decreasing unit sales provide an early warning signal that can be addressed now rather than later—when dollar volume sales begin to drop as well.

Making It Happen

List all the types of products you sold last year in the far left column of Worksheet 2.2. Then tabulate the actual number of units you sold for each type of product by month. Add the total units by product in the first shaded column. In the last column, divide this number by 12 to get the average unit sales by month.

Now do this worksheet a second time to project the number of units you expect to sell this year. Project as conservatively as possible. If you do not have a specific reason to expect an increase, use last year's average numbers as a projection. In some products, you probably expect a decrease. There may also be new products to add that you did not have last year. Factor these differences into your projections.

You can also apply a percentage increase to the number of units sold last year to get a projection for this year, although this tends to be less

Worksheet 2.2
Unit Sales by Product

☐ Actuals Last Year
☐ Projections for This Year
☐ Actuals for This Year

Product	Month												Unit Sales Year-to-Date	Average Unit Sales by Month*
	1	2	3	4	5	6	7	8	9	10	11	12		

*Divide total year-to-date unit sales by current month number.

accurate than estimating what you will sell month to month based on marketing efforts. Finally, Worksheet 2.2 can be used to monitor how close your actual unit sales are to your projections by adding the actual numbers to a third blank worksheet.

Reality Check

Consider these questions about your completed worksheet:

- Are unit sales cyclical as evidenced by sharp increases in certain months or seasons?

- Are unit increases due to particular marketing efforts?

- Are unit sales obviously affected by particular accounts' buying patterns?

- Are new products doing as well as expected as soon as expected?

- Have any product sales dwindled during the year or from the past year?

DOLLAR SALES PROJECTIONS BY PRODUCT

Worksheet 2.3 helps you project, conservatively, the dollar sales using unit projections by product with an average selling price from the prior year.

It is important for the morale of the company to be aggressive in marketing and to have high expectations of the sales growth you want to achieve. Save these high hopes for your sales meetings. The budgeting process considers both sales and expenses. If you project a 20 percent increase in sales for the purpose of determining your profit picture, you may allow yourself to increase your expenses by more than you should.

While the company is busy looking at what it is spending, the sales and marketing people must be busy looking also at what the expected sales are. Take a very conservative approach to sales projections. Base them as much as possible on what actually happened the prior year, both in terms of real unit sales and your actual average selling prices. Factor in any price increases and expected unit increases very carefully.

Remember, in virtually all but the most disciplined companies, if sales are up, people ease up on the expense reins and the horse runs free. Almost all employees can find something they would like to have to improve their lot. If money appears to be no object, people will ask for more than they really need—including everything from office furniture to computer software.

Making It Happen

Because the most realistic sales projections are done by looking not at dollars, but at units sold, we begin with the unit sales number from the previous worksheet (2.2). The number of units projected to be sold is then multiplied by the average price received for the product last year to get an idea of what sales dollars the product would be expected to bring in this year.

It is also important to factor in any price increases, but be very conservative in doing so. If you increase your selling price by 10 percent, often you don't increase your discounted price to high volume purchasers by an equal amount. In this case, you might want to factor in only a 5 percent increase in the average price.

Worksheet 2.3
Dollar Sales Projections by Product

A Product	B* Unit Sales by Product	C** Average Price per Product	D Projected Price Increases (%)	Projected $ Sales (B/C/D)

*From Unit Sales by Product Worksheet.
**From Average Price per Product Worksheet.

To get a total, multiply columns B, C, and D of Worksheet 2.3. The shaded box at the bottom should be your total expected dollar sales for the entire year.

Reality Check

Consider these questions about completed Worksheet 2.3:

- Have you reviewed profitability and market factors to consider price increases?

- Are projected sales substantially greater or less than actual sales from last year?

- Are sales projections particularly aggressive for some products and not for others? Do these differences accurately reflect the positions of various products in their sales cycles?

- Are there other significant sources of income not taken into account by product sales (i.e., shipping and handling)?

- Is there any other information, such as the possible loss of a major customer, that needs to be factored into sales projections?

DOLLAR SALES PROJECTIONS BY MONTH

Worksheet 2.4 takes the dollar sales projections developed on the prior worksheet and allocates them by month by looking at sales by month during the prior year. It is important to know when we expect the sales to be booked. For most companies, sales are recorded on shipment of the company's product.

Filling in Worksheet 2.4 with your actual sales figures from the previous year will allow you to see if any of your products are seasonal. Even if sales of your products generally don't appear to have any dramatic fluctuations from month to month, certain products will. This may signal a particular buying segment that orders at a particular time of year. Knowing this may help you spend your marketing dollars for this buying group at the right time.

Making It Happen

For the purpose of accurate projections, it is important to do Worksheet 2.4 twice.

First, use actual numbers from the last full year to get the percentages that are calculated at the bottom of the page. These numbers show what percentage of the total sales was made each month of the previous 12 months. The total in the box at the bottom right should be 100 percent.

List your products in the left-hand column. List actual dollar sales by product for each of the past 12 months. Total the numbers, month by month, at the bottom of the page. Using these total dollar figures, divide the total dollars by month by the total dollars in the shaded box at the bottom right corner. Enter these percentages by month at the bottom of each column.

For your second calculation, use the totals and percentages you just calculated at the bottom of the first Dollar Sales Projections by Product Worksheet (2.3) to make sales projections. This time, enter the total dollars by product that you calculated in the previous worksheet (from Dollar Sales Projections by Product [2.3]) in the far right column, and total at the bottom. Next, enter the percentages by month at the bottom of the page from the percentages done on the worksheet showing the actual numbers from last year. Multiply the number in the total column by the percentage at the

Worksheet 2.4
Dollar Sales Projections by Month

☐ Actuals Last Year
☐ Projections This Year

Product	Month 1	2	3	4	5	6	7	8	9	10	11	12	Total*
Product	$	$	$	$	$	$	$	$	$	$	$	$	$
% by Month	%	%	%	%	%	%	%	%	%	%	%	%	100%

* From Dollar Sales Projections by Product worksheet for this year only.

bottom to get a number to fill in each box. This will give you an expected dollar sales volume by month.

Illustrating this data graphically (a simple bar chart works well) will increase its impact.

Reality Check

Consider these questions about your completed worksheet:

- What effect does seasonality have on sales and cash flow?

- How do debt service and other major financial commitments coincide with or run counter to the annual sales cycle? How will this affect your cash flow?

- Will profit margin decrease substantially because of variable costs coming into play during certain times of the year?

- Can marketing efforts be adjusted to smooth out erratic cyclical and seasonal sales patterns?

- Will you require a line of credit or some other borrowing mechanism if cash flow isn't adequate to meet expenses during certain times of the year? Is that borrowing mechanism ready?

EXPENSE BUDGETING

I'm convinced that there is only one way to start to review your expenses and project your sales: from the bottom up and in writing. Many companies project expenses by increasing each expense item by a regular annual percentage or budget as a percentage of sales. In contrast, a bottom-up method forces you essentially to start over each year.

This allows more flexibility to do things such as reducing expenses. When you carefully analyze the checks you write, you may find you're paying for things you aren't using, especially for ongoing commitments such as maintenance agreements. An annual review is essential.

In preparing for your annual review, it goes without saying that the number-crunching part of the budgeting process can and should be done by computer, but spreadsheets are only a part of a budget. The "whys" for the numbers are often contained in peripheral documents such as leases or supplier purchase agreements. To understand the budget completely, you should house the spreadsheets and copies of relevant documents together. Putting the interim and final product in a notebook allows for easy access and discussion at meetings and for reference during the year, and it makes a much more accessible and complete document for employees. It also allows an obvious place for note taking to prepare for the next year's budget process.

Spreadsheets can be set up by department on a computer network, giving each manager a password for access to his or her department's section only. These sections can automatically be added to the total company worksheet so that changes will total immediately.

THE BUDGET NOTEBOOK

Our company created a budget notebook each year that documented every expense item, including which suppliers we had used and general ledger numbers to correctly categorize each expense. The importance of complete documentation in your budgeting process cannot be overemphasized:

- First, the budgeting exercise in this book makes you really analyze your sales projections and expenses in detail. It doesn't allow you to pass over any item.

- Second, it tells your accounting department how you want items categorized for reporting purposes. You may wonder why rents are so high on your reports. It may be because accounting thinks you want equipment rents expense reported here, while you think accounting allocates this expense to repairs and maintenance. With documentation, everyone is clear on which expense goes where.

- Third, it will convince your employees, like nothing else, that you mean business about really scrutinizing what is being spent.

Done well, the budget notebook can be the one place to find all the answers. You can keep copies of contracts in this notebook to show expense commitments you have made for periods beyond the current year. Last, this kind of notebook helps employees understand how the company's money is being spent. Employees sometimes overestimate—significantly—how much the owner or manager takes out of a business. They assume that if you take in $3 million in revenue, the owner is taking home $2 million. The notebook shows them how much money it takes to make payroll, pay insurance premiums, pay rent, and so on.

Set up your notebook in a three-ring binder. Prepare the dividers and have one blank sheet of paper for each item with its title on the top. To begin writing, start with the easiest items first, usually some recurring, consistent expenses. For example, how much do you pay in rent each month? Add to this any information you need about your lease, such as the starting and ending dates, and when increases occur. This is a good time to review your lease and look for any hidden costs that will need to be a part of your budget.

Each line item has several general ledger account numbers associated with it. These general ledger numbers are used by your accounting staff to allocate every item for which the company writes checks. By looking at each of the expenditures in each general ledger account number, you can do budgeting from the bottom up. Ask your accounting department to add your general ledger numbers to the right side of this sheet.

Try to use the "miscellaneous" line item as little as possible. I never budget for anything other than petty cash in this category so it will not become a catchall for items accounting cannot otherwise categorize.

The budget notebook starts with sales projections, which we focused on in the last few worksheets. Your sales divider should be followed by the completed Average Selling Price Per Product Worksheet (2.1), the Unit Sales by Product Worksheet (2.2), the Dollar Sales Projections by Product (2.3), and by Month worksheets (2.4). These will give you a system to calculate conservative expectations of sales by which you can realistically budget expenses.

We had four other sections that called for dividers in our notebook:

1. *Cost of goods sold.* The expenses incurred in making your product.

2. *Sales and marketing expenses.* What it costs you to sell your product.

3. *Overhead expenses.* Most of the other expenses incurred in operating an office.

4. *Income taxes.* We don't discuss estimating taxes in this book, but you should have a section in your notebook for tax planning and discuss this with your CPA.

In addition, we had a section for the balance sheet budget, which includes major capital expenditures. In the following index from our budget notebook, the categories in bold type are section topics and have their own sections, and each line item listed has its own page. Every company will have its own additional items, but what follows are the main categories that are almost universal:

Sales projections.

Cost of goods sold.
Materials purchased.
Salaries and wages.
Production supplies.
Temporary help.
Shipping supplies.
Mailing and shipping.

Sales and marketing expenses.
Salaries.
Sales commissions.
Direct mail.
Advertising.
Publicity.
Consulting.
Other sales and marketing expenses.

Overhead expenses.
Personnel.
Salaries.
Bonuses.
Payroll taxes.
Group life and health insurance.
Workers compensation insurance.
Employee benefit plans.
Officers' salaries.
Employment expense.
Training.
Temporary help.

Facilities.
Rents.
Property tax.
Repairs and maintenance.

Utilities.
Property and liability insurance.

Administration.
Accounting services.
Automobiles.
Bank charges.
Computer supplies.
Charitable contributions.
Depreciation and amortization.
Dues and subscriptions.
Legal services.
Licenses.
Miscellaneous.
Office supplies.
Other professional services.
Telephone.
Travel.

Income taxes.

Making It Happen

This process gives you a format for writing down and tracking expected expense items, as well as a way to compare last year's expected and actual numbers for the same group of expenses. Worksheet 2.5 is an example of what a budget notebook page might look like. I've provided a sample of a page titled "Rents," which might include office building leases, parking, warehousing, and equipment rentals. Start by listing, at the bottom of the page, what the budget and actual numbers were for the previous year. This will give you an idea of what the expense figure for this year might be and whether there is a tendency to over- or underbudget for this item.

The Rents category may include several general ledger accounts—office space rental, equipment rental, or warehouse rentals. For each of these general ledger account numbers, your accounting department should have a standard list of vendors to whom they often write checks. Ask to see this standard list on a regular basis.

Again, budgeting should be a participative process. Doing it alone defeats the purpose. Teams should be given the responsibility to analyze last year's bills and project expenditures by category and vendor this year.

Worksheet 2.5
Sample Expense Budget Page

		2004
Rents		
Main Building	ABC Properties ($16,198/month, increases 3% on 8/1)	$196,806
Parking	Parking Lots, Inc. (12 spaces at $40/month)	480
Warehouse	SuperStorage ($200/month)	2,400
Equipment Rentals		
Postage Meter Rental	Pitney Bowes ($412.50 twice a year, due 1/1 and 7/1)	835
Copy Machines	Xerox ($356/month, expires 4/4/07)	4,272
Telephone	Bell Communications ($1,219/month, expires 7/1/08)	14,628
TOTAL:		$219,421
Budget Last Year:		$195,008
Actual Last Year:		$201,962

Especially once you have been through the process a year or two, teams should report to you annually on ways to reduce these expenses, and management's role during the process should be limited to making final decisions on approving expenditures and to putting it all together to get the desired profit picture.

On each blank sheet, first list the type of item. Next to each, list the vendor of that item. Last, make an estimate of how much you think you will spend on that item this year. This estimate can be made by looking at how much you spent last year and making an educated guess as to whether this will go up or down. You can also often get a close to actual number if the item is based on a contractual agreement and doesn't often vary. Be sure to consider automatic price increase clauses and other hidden costs often overlooked. Wherever possible in this budget, list the important financial points of the lease to make this process easier next year and to let the accounting department know if these payments are expected to increase, stop, or decrease at any point during the year.

Reality Check

Consider these questions about your budget notebook:

- Have all important expense items been captured in the worksheet? Does your budgeting process include most, if not all, employees? Do you feel certain you have captured all your real expenses?

- Have you reviewed supplier contracts or other agreements to capture all costs and look for cost reduction possibilities?

- Are your preliminary estimates significantly over or under the actual numbers for last year?

- Are explanatory notes understandable to everyone?

- Are there any items you are no longer using?

- Are there any numbers that seem out of proportion to the value of the service you are paying for?

- Look at total amounts paid to various vendors during the previous full year. Will this year be about the same as last? Is there an automatic increase to any of these expenses?

- Do you plan to use less of a given product or service next year?

- Do you always pay a specific amount for a given product or service each month, or does it vary by the quantity used?

- Are there new vendors you're negotiating with now that you plan to begin using in the near future? How will they compare with existing expense items?

- Are your expense categories all encompassing? Would all of your suppliers' services fit into some category?

- Will the categories you have chosen be meaningful in decision making?

- Do some of these categories house too many different types of items so it won't be clear to all what the category means?

PAYROLL PROJECTIONS

Worksheet 2.6 will accurately project and document payroll, the largest area of expense for most companies. It is important to project payroll accurately, not only because it is a significant expense in and of itself, but also because of its direct impact on many other expense categories. Payroll taxes, workers' compensation insurance, life and disability insurance, and retirement plan expenses generally all fluctuate with changes in payroll.

This worksheet will help you to look at how payroll is spread out over time. Most entrepreneurs know exactly which weeks they need to cover their payrolls. It's hard for most employees to understand, but if your payroll is $1 million a year (and a company of 35 people can easily have that), every two weeks the company sends out about $40,000 worth of paychecks.

My company paid employees every other Friday, which came to 26 paychecks a year. Employees got three paychecks in June and December, and two in every other month. Accordingly, our payroll on a cash basis was higher in June and December than in every other month. This becomes important to know if June is your lowest sales month.

Finally, if there is one piece of most budgets to which not everyone has access, that piece is the payroll. This makes it difficult to study for cost reduction as openly as you might any other budget item.

Making It Happen

To calculate payroll, ask each manager to determine the department's head count and payroll costs. Worksheet 2.6 gives columns for each employee's current salary (times a number of months) plus a column for a salary increase (times the number of months the higher salary will be in effect).

Adding the numbers in the last column gives you the total compensation of each department's employees for the year. Add below the actual payroll for that department last year. Totaling the shaded box at the bottom right of each department worksheet will give you the total company payroll.

Payroll is rarely, if ever, reduced, except in crises. Employees never expect their salaries to be static. They generally expect their compensation

Worksheet 2.6
Payroll Projections

Employee #	Employee Name	Current Monthly Salary*	× # of Months	= Total at Current Salary	Next Salary Increase (Date)	x % Increase	Future Salary*	× # of Months	= Total at New Salary	TOTAL COMPENSATION (Total Shaded Columns)
										Total

Actual Total for Last Year $ _____

*If hourly wage, convert to monthly. Formula to convert hourly rate to monthly rate is: Hourly rate × 173.3 (example $10 hr × 173.3 = $1733/month).

to increase once a year. These increases rarely respond to real productivity increases. They're part of an entitlement employees feel about their jobs, which most assume include a higher salary and greater benefits with each passing year.

Because of the always-growing nature of payrolls, many companies are experimenting with progressive compensation plans, including performance-based pay. Regardless of how you determine what you pay your employees, payroll must be projected to get an accurate profit picture.

Reality Check

Consider these questions about your payroll projections:

- Are some departments' payrolls increasing more quickly than others? Is this because of additions to staff or pay increases? Is this in line with your overall growth plans?

- Are your payroll dollars going to the areas you wish to emphasize?

- Are managers realistic about the increases they want to give?

- How much has your total payroll increased this year? In dollars? As a percentage? How will this affect other expenses?

- Is your compensation competitive for your industry?

- Do you check at least annually for internal equity in your compensation system?

- Do some months require significantly more dollars to meet payroll than others?

- Is it possible to stagger pay increases throughout the year?

- Are salary dollars predominantly spent for employees making and selling the products, or is a lot more spent on administrative overhead?

- Is your projected head count higher or lower than last year? How will that influence other expenses?

INCOME STATEMENT PROJECTIONS

This exercise pulls together on one page (see Worksheet 2.7) all the items gathered in the budget notebook and looks overall at your profit picture. Categorizing your expenses this way is important to begin to look at your overall profit picture as a number you can control.

Making It Happen

From the information gathered in the budget notebook, you can begin to analyze your profit picture by putting your numbers in four major categories as follows:

1. *Cost of goods sold* includes the direct costs that go into producing your product. The percentage in the box next to this category is the complement of your gross profit margin. In other words, if cost of goods sold percentage is 69 percent, gross profit margin is 31 percent.

2. *Sales and marketing expenses* include what it costs to market and sell your product. In some cases, it costs more than the price of the product to sell it, and only in repeat business is there a reasonable profit margin. It is important to know so that you can price accordingly.

3. *Overhead expenses* include all other items such as personnel not in other categories, facilities costs, and administrative items such as office supplies.

4. The *net income* at the bottom of Worksheet 2.7 should be a budget item, just like the rest of your expenses. I'm not satisfied unless this number is at least 15 percent, but this varies by your industry and economic times.

To obtain the current year projection (the shaded column), enter the total number from each budget notebook page you filled out for each category. For sales, enter the projection for this year and the actual for last year from the Dollar Sales Projections by Month Worksheet 2.4 (shaded box on bottom right for both years). For other categories, enter the projection number from each budget notebook page and the actual numbers from the previous year that you added to each budget notebook page.

Worksheet 2.7
Income Statement Projections

Notebook Item	Current Year Projection	% of Sales	Actual Last Year	% of Sales	Fixed (F) or Variable (V)?
Sales					
Cost of Goods Sold					
Beginning Inventory					
Materials purchased					
Salaries & wages					
Production supplies					
Temporary help					
Shipping supplies					
Mailing & shipping					
Less Ending Inventory					
Total Cost of Goods Sold					
Gross Profit (Sales – total cost of goods sold)					
Gross Profit % (Gross Profit / Sales)					
Sales & Marketing Expenses					
Salaries					
Sales commissions					
Direct mail					
Advertising					
Publicity					
Consulting					
Other sales & marketing expenses					
Total Sales & Marketing Expenses					
Overhead Expenses					
Personnel					
Salaries					
Bonuses					
Payroll taxes					
Group life & health insurance					
Workers compensation insurance					
Employee benefit plans					

Worksheet 2.7 (Continued)

Notebook Item	Current Year Projection	% of Sales	Actual Last Year	% of Sales	Fixed (F) or Variable (V)?
Officers' salaries					
Employment expense					
Training					
Temporary help					
Total Personnel					
Facilities					
Rents					
Property tax					
Repairs & maintenance					
Utilities					
Property & liability insurance					
Total Facilities					
Administration					
Accounting services					
Automobiles					
Bank charges					
Computer supplies					
Charitable contributions					
Depreciation & amortization					
Dues & subscriptions					
Interest expense					
Legal services					
Licenses					
Miscellaneous					
Office supplies					
Other professional services					
Telephone					
Travel					
Total Administration					
Total Overhead Expenses					
Income (before taxes)					
Income Taxes					
Net Income					

Calculate the percentage of your total sales that each category makes up by dividing the total number at the bottom of each box by the total sales box at the top. You should have percentages for each of the items except sales.

The last column of Worksheet 2.7 requires that you determine whether your costs are fixed or variable. *Variable costs* are costs that are directly impacted by sales. These costs are expected to change, more or less, in proportion to the change in sales, for example, sales commissions. *Fixed costs* are all those that are not variable—they don't change as the level of sales increases or decreases. An example of this is rent. Some costs may have both a variable piece and a fixed piece, for example, utilities, which go up as equipment is used more to meet production demands but are relatively fixed for most of the office. For purposes of this analysis, expenses that are in doubt should be classified as fixed.

Reality Check

Consider these questions about your income statement projections:

- Are you satisfied with the dollar number and the percentage at the bottom of the page?

- Are these numbers higher or lower than the previous year?

- Compare these percentages with industry norms. Are you higher or lower than others in your industry?

- Are category totals as a percentage of sales higher or lower than you would expect?

- Have you questioned numbers that seem wrong to you? Do you have backup calculations or information for all the numbers?

BALANCE SHEET PROJECTIONS

A balance sheet is a statement of what the company owns and what it owes at a fixed point in time. The balance sheet can be illustrated by a simple formula with three elements:

Assets − Liabilities = Owner's equity

Making It Happen

Make a list of your assets and liabilities in the following categories. Assets can be current, fixed, or intangible. Liabilities can be short or long term. What your business is worth or how much value you have built up in the business is the owner's equity.

Assets

Current Assets

- Your cash.

- Cash from loans or investors.

- Inventory—list type and value.

- Deposits paid upfront (such as rent and security).

- Other expenses paid upfront to be used over time (such as annual insurance premiums).

- Accounts receivable—credit you give to others who will buy from you now and pay later.

Fixed Assets

- Real property.

- Improvements to your location.

- Equipment.

Intangible Assets

- Intellectual property rights—copyrights, trademarks, patents (list type and estimated value).

Liabilities

Current Liabilities (less than two years to pay back)

- Notes payable (such as bank lines of credit and equipment loans that will be fully paid back in less than two years).

- Credit given to you to buy what you need now and pay later (accounts payable).

Long-Term Debt (more than two years to full repayment)

- Bank Loans.

Owner's Equity

If your assets are greater than your liabilities, you have equity or worth in your business that you should list on your balance sheet projections. If your liabilities are greater than your assets, you have negative equity. Many businesses start with negative equity, but all businesses should seek to increase equity each year.

Reality Check

Consider these questions about your balance sheet projections:

- Are your assets greater than your liabilities?

- Over the life of your business, have your assets increased or decreased?

- Over the life of your business, have your liabilities increased or decreased?

- What is the owner's equity of your business? Has it increased? Do you have a goal for how much you would like your business to be worth?

BREAK-EVEN ANALYSIS

Worksheet 2.8 determines the sales level at which the company neither makes a profit nor suffers a loss. Break-even analysis can help to identify problems and avoid or lessen losses by acting proactively rather than reactively. Obviously, the sooner you recognize that the company is operating at less than break-even operations, the sooner you can begin to cut fixed costs and take other measures to restore profitability.

Some companies use break-even analysis to evaluate their overall profit goal. It is a simple-to-use tool to relate sales to profit. Break-even analysis is driven by the relationship of costs, volumes, and profits.

Break-even analysis offers a consistent way to test proposed transactions, consider alternatives, or make decisions. Most of the information required to determine your break-even already exists in your annual budget.

Making It Happen

Use the previous Income Statement Projections Worksheet (2.7) to determine which costs are fixed and which are variable. For Part I of Worksheet 2.8, determine the variable cost percentage by one of two ways:

1. Divide the total variable costs by projected sales.

$$\frac{\text{Variable cost}}{\text{Sales}} = \text{Variable cost percentage}$$

2. Using historical financial statements, divide all variable costs by sales to derive each variable cost as a percentage of sales. Then add all of these percentages to obtain a total variable cost percentage.

Example:

Materials:	50 percent
Production:	10 percent
Direct labor:	10 percent
Sales salaries:	15 percent
Total variable cost:	75 percent

Worksheet 2.8
Break-Even Analysis

Part I

	% of Sales[a]
Variable Expenses	
Materials purchased	
Production supplies	
Shipping supplies	
Mailing & shipping	
Sales commissions	
Total Variable Cost %	**%**
Contribution Margin Ratio (100% minus the total variable cost %)	%
Fixed Costs	
Monthly	$
Annual	$
Break-Even Sales Level	
Monthly	$
Annual	$

Part II

Fixed Expenses	Annual[b]	Monthly[c]
Personnel	$	$
Salaries & wages – Cost of sales		
Salaries – Administration		
Bonuses		
Payroll taxes		
Group life & health insurance		
Workers compensation insurance		
Employee benefit plans		
Officers' salaries		
Employment expense		
Training		
Temporary help		
Total Personnel Costs	$	$

Worksheet 2.8 (Continued)

	Annual[b]	Monthly[c]
Sales & Marketing Expenses		
Salaries		
Sales commissions		
Direct mail		
Advertising		
Publicity		
Consulting		
Other sales & marketing expenses		
Total Sales & Marketing Expenses	$	$
Facilities		
Rents		
Property tax		
Repairs & maintenance		
Utilities		
Property & liability insurance		
Total Facilities	$	$
Administration		
Accounting services		
Automobiles		
Bank charges		
Computer supplies		
Charitable contributions		
Depreciation & amortization		
Dues & subscriptions		
Interest expense		
Legal services		
Licenses		
Miscellaneous		
Office supplies		
Other professional services		
Telephone		
Travel		
Total Administration	$	$
Total Fixed Expenses	$	$

[a] From *Income Statement Projections* worksheet (2.7), current year projection, % of sales column for variable expenses only.

[b] From *Income Statement Projections* worksheet (2.7), current year projections column.

[c] Current year projections divided by 12.

The goal of Part II is to determine the contribution margin ratio to add back into Part I. This ratio is calculated by taking the complement of the variable cost percentage or simply by subtracting the variable cost percentage from 100 percent.

$$\text{Contribution margin ratio} = 100 \text{ percent} - \text{Variable cost percent}$$

Now you are ready to calculate sales break-even level. To do this, divide total fixed costs by the contribution margin ratio.

$$\text{Sales break-even level} = \frac{\text{Total fixed costs}}{\text{Contribution margin ratio}}$$

Reality Check

Consider these questions about your break-even analysis:

- If sales begin to decline, at what level will you start to lose money?

- If you increase fixed costs by $X, how much additional sales will you need to generate to cover these costs?

- If you lower the variable cost percentage, what impact will it have on profits?

- If you want a profit of $X, what level of sales will you have to achieve?

- Are there months where your projections are less than break-even on sales?

WHAT'S NEXT

In the next chapter, I cover how to look at what really happens after you complete the budget and go back to business. I discuss how you can interpret financial data to ensure your company is on the right track. I also cover how to share financial information and budget requirements with your employees and how to make this information relevant and useful to them.

3

UNDERSTANDING THE NUMBERS

The expectations of life depend upon diligence; the mechanic that would perfect his work must first sharpen his tools.

—Confucious

A primary goal of every business is to make enough money to stay in business. Making money can be defined in two ways: making a profit and generating cash. Profitable businesses usually generate cash, but not always. Unprofitable businesses sometimes generate cash, but not often.

Either way, in reviewing your finances, you look at both profits and cash. This chapter takes you through this review by stressing three points:

1. The importance of tracking variances from budgeted amounts.

2. The importance of cash in running any business.

3. The central role of developing key financial indicators and communicating them to coworkers.

Choosing your key financial indicators depends on the kind of business you run and whether your company is young or mature. As a rule, cash is king for a young company; many start-up owners fear running out of cash more than anything else. In a mature company, sales and growth may become the main concern. When a company goes public, showing a good return on assets may become paramount.

FLYING BLIND

The owners of many new businesses fly blind, concentrating on the day-to-day essentials at the expense of reviewing the numbers and planning ahead. Once they start reviewing and planning, they discover that the process brings unexpected payoffs in reaching their goals because it forces them to identify what they want and to determine the means by which to get there. Effective managers develop their own methods for gauging performance, and they define performance in accordance with their short- and long-term goals. They may consider daily revenues, for example, or catalogs mailed, cash balance, and payroll.

The small business owner must become intimately involved in the daily dynamics of the business. This familiarity provides a long-term blue-print for keeping the company vital because the key to implementation is in the details.

Essential Financial Measurements

The following are six essential measurements of financial well-being for most businesses:

1. *Revenue dollars.* Are total sales up or down for the period?

2. *Gross profit margin percentage.* One of the profit indicators you look at first, this measurement takes into account only the costs directly related to the product manufactured.

3. *Net income.* Always a key indicator of financial performance, net income reflects sales and costs, profit and loss—the best places to start any analysis.

4. *Cash position.* Especially in the early years of a company's his-tory, liquidity has more importance than any other financial benchmark. But whatever the maturity of your company, it pays to watch how much money you have in the bank at least weekly and maybe even daily. If you have a line of credit, how much of the line is in use and how much is available becomes an impor-tant part of your available cash calculation.

5. *Net worth.* This indicator, which tells the owner's equity (or in publicly traded companies, shareholders' equity), is simply assets minus liabilities. It includes equity put into the business through

the sale of stock or retained earnings. It helps you consider the best ways to allocate equity and assets to reach your goals.

6. *Accounts payable days and accounts receivable days.* Many experts call these *leading indicators* because they give you a read on what your cash position will be next month. However, accounts receivable are sometimes collected more slowly than payables come due, in which case your cash position might become tight.

Your management of receivables and payables profoundly affects cash flow. Poor management here can kill almost any company, no matter what the size, and good management pays big dividends.

Just by managing receivables well, even in a small company, you can generate tremendous amounts of cash—in today's volatile economy—and this is essential.

Another way to look at the receivables/payables ratio is as a measure of your financial department's efficiency. Your accounting people must make sure the company pays its bills and collects its receivables on time.

TRADITIONAL FINANCIAL STATEMENTS

The traditional financial statement has two components—the income statement and the balance sheet. The *income statement* shows your sales and expenses and profit and loss for a given period, usually the month, quarter, or year. The *balance sheet* shows net worth; it also details items such as inventory, fixed assets, accounts payable, and accounts receivable.

Another important financial statement, not always prepared by small companies, is a *statement of cash flows.* This statement shows the details of how cash increased or decreased during the period and where it went.

Make sure financials are prepared monthly, preferably by the tenth of the following month at the latest. Learn which pieces of information in them are relevant to your business and concentrate on those. Don't ignore what the numbers tell you and, above all, believe them; good or bad, the numbers are important. In addition, don't hesitate to shape the reports you get to suit your ends. Accountants tend to work by habit, and they sometimes prepare numbers for business managers without giving much thought to making them truly useful. You need to make sure the reports you get are truly useful for making decisions about your business.

In all cases, your financial statements look backward to show the present—namely, your position as of their date of preparation. Finally, don't forget, if you have a bank loan, the bankers will be looking at these numbers as well to make sure you can pay off your debt.

Setting Your Own Key Indicators

Implicit in this discussion is the fact that your concentration on the financial statements may blind you to opportunity. Budgets set cost targets, leading some managers to spend their time controlling how much the operation spends and ignoring how much it earns now or might make in the future. They monitor money going out, and they don't take into account issues such as trends, the big picture, or the business underlying the profit and loss statement, which shows results. Worse, they ignore the balance sheet, which shows your financial position.

This single-mindedness can hamper your business. It turns an organization inward, values rule above initiative, and lead managers to query trivial variances while they ignore harder-to-identify, companywide problems or opportunities.

Therefore, financial measurements must always be balanced against measures of operations, product development, and marketing.

One way to counteract this is to develop specific *key indicators* for your business. A key indicator answers the questions: How well are we really doing? If you were managing the business in crisis mode and you had to focus only on the essentials, what would you need to know? What numbers or other data would you want on your desk every morning? It is worth spending significant time identifying your business's true key indicators and making sure you have that data available to you consistently.

CASH FLOW IS CRITICAL

Many small business owners don't think about all the strategies and tools available to them when they run into cash flow problems. Instead, they react by trying to boost sales. They chase revenue, and cost is damned. In so doing, they overextend themselves seeking new business and fail to serve their best customers. This can harm cash flow—the last thing a company needs if liquidity is already a problem.

There are several strategies for maximizing cash flow. Controlling expenses is chief among them.

Many business owners see expense controls as a sign of trouble, but they aren't. The *absence* of cost controls is a sign of trouble.

If you find your business short of cash, look to your balance sheet and study receivables and inventory, both of which are common drains on cash flow.

Managing Your Receivables

It is important to carefully track customers who bought your company's product on credit but haven't paid as they have agreed to within a specific time. The older the bills get, the less likely they will be paid.

It's essential for managers to have a plan to get people to pay, and the first step in that is to know who owes money, how long they've owed it, and how much they owe. Sometimes the top 20 can account for most of the money owed to a company if it has several large customers.

Doing something as simple as concentrating on getting paid by these people can have a significant impact on raising a company's cash position. Consider keeping a list of the customers who owe you money and rank them from the largest dollar volume to the smallest. Enter the top 10, from largest to smallest on this worksheet. Keep track of their payments and who is responsible for contacting them. What percentage do your top 20 receivables represent of accounts receivable? Are any of the customers on the list still buying on credit? Do you have limits as to how much credit you will allow?

Perhaps the best use of accounts receivable days and payable days as a management tool is to compare the two. Average the time it takes to pay your bills and the time it takes to collect. If it takes longer to collect accounts receivable than pay your bills, in effect, you're subsidizing customers. If it takes longer to pay than collect, you're effectively making money from the process.

WITH RECEIVABLES, A FEW BASIC RULES APPLY:

- Develop a good credit-checking system.

- Send your bills out faster, and follow up with phone calls when an account becomes overdue.

- Establish a strict collections schedule and follow it faithfully.

- If your cash flow is strong, you may be willing to give extra time to pay in exchange for additional compensation.

- Keep managers and employees informed when collections become difficult with products they develop, make, or sell. They may help with strategies for collecting. They may also know something useful about the customer that will help in collection efforts.

- Don't be afraid to pick up the phone and call the company president.

- Don't wait too long to get attorneys involved if all else fails. A legal letter and some minimal action can often bring about quick payment.

Managing Your Inventory

Another cash drain is excess inventory. Without adequate controls over receivables and inventory, it's entirely possible for a company to make a profit and still go out of business. Whenever and as much as possible, you should integrate inventory management with customer service and delivery programs. The object is to keep as few units on warehouse shelves as you can.

The cost of carrying inventory is expensive. Some manufacturing companies pay 25 to 30 percent of the value of their inventory for the cost of borrowed money, warehouse space, materials handling, staff, and transportation expenses related to maintaining it for one financial quarter—three months.

These numbers shock people. Once they realize how expensive inventory can be, they look at it differently. Many owners and managers never

SCRUPULOUS MONITORING

Unity Forest Products, Inc., a California-based lumber company, thrives by scrupulously monitoring its cash flow and related items such as inventory, accounts receivable, and accounts payable. In a volatile business, it combines efficiency, knowledge of its customers' needs, and close attention to financial detail to succeed.

Unity started as a bootstrap operation run by a collection of long-time mill workers who didn't fear competing with the industry's big players. Lumber is a heavily capitalized, low margin business, and bootstrappers don't usually have the money to get in the game. CEO Enita Elphick and her crew needed $1 million to get started. In 1987, when starting out, the management team had only $350,000 in cash. For a short time, Unity bought lumber from sawmills, subcontracted the resawing, and then sold the wood wholesale to lumberyards.

Elphick had refined a just-in-time inventory management concept into a five-year business plan that depended on weekly cash flow projections—unusual for any start-up, let alone one in a volatile commodity business. Unity claimed it could turn inventory over every 10 days; the industry average was 58. The company also claimed it could collect accounts receivable in 10 days; the industry average was 27.

Management looked everywhere for cash to build a new mill but had trouble persuading lenders to back its plan, which lenders considered so aggressive that they doubted its projections. Wells Fargo approved a $150,000 credit line that Unity never touched. Finally, the bank lent Unity the cash to get started.

Elphick offers her customers a 1 percent discount if they pay within 10 days. In turn, it gets a 2 percent discount from suppliers if Unity pays within 10 days. Competitors see that Unity has figured out that the most significant expense in the lumber industry is carrying a lot of inventory.

Unity also keeps close track of receivables. At one point, a customer who owed the company $40,000 was about to declare bankruptcy. Unity managers drove several company trucks to the customer's plant and repossessed the lumber before sheriff's deputies could arrive to lock up the facility. This tenacity and attention to detail is in part what makes this company thrive.

make this realization because the cost doesn't show up on any statement, and, therefore, they have to calculate it themselves.

FOLLOWING WHAT MATTERS

There's nothing like a brush with disaster to show you what matters and what doesn't, as the Wisconsin-based Carson Pirie Scott department store chain learned during a bankruptcy reorganization in 1991. The exercise taught management to improve performance by paying close attention to the company's real-time financial position, which is key in retailing with its turnover and stiff competition.

Michael MacDonald, then chief financial officer, tracked sales and cash position on a weekly basis. As he said, "You really have to manage a business on a detailed basis and on a frequent basis. You don't just look at it now and again. You have to look at it all the time—every day."

The company used a five-inch-thick business plan to chart its way out of bankruptcy. Its creditors insisted that the retailer remain wary of variances from budget. The business plan became the company's road map away from disaster. "There's an axiom in retail that says retail is detail," MacDonald says. "You need to track sales on hand on a very detailed basis. We have pretty sophisticated methods to check what sizes and colors are selling."

For key indicators, managers chart sales per square foot, comparable-store sales growth (to show market share), and operating profit as a percentage of sales and earnings.

As MacDonald points out, cash and inventory "require continuous fine tuning and monitoring." The challenge is to make sure that the shortage of cash doesn't choke off the flow of in-demand products.

He describes the goal of his financial scorekeeping bluntly: "The main purpose of a business is to maximize shareholder or investor value." He watched a number of indicators to achieve that end, all tied to what the company called the *three keys to successful retailing*—effective merchandising, giving the customer a positive shopping experience, and marketing.

The attention to detail paid off. Within two years, Carson Pirie Scott had earnings of about $33 million on sales of $1.15 billion—not stellar numbers, but on target with management's goals to avert disaster. By 1998, it had become an acquisition target, and its 55 stores became part of Saks, Inc.

When Numbers Lag Performance

One key to the success of the Carson Pirie Scott effort was its ability to limit an important shortcoming in financial analysis—the fact that the numbers lag actual performance. For example, the company knew that if it tracked expenses only at the end of each quarter, it would do so too late to make a difference.

The financials also can't answer qualitative questions such as those that go into the formulation of your company's vision statement. In addition, you may well find that your financial statement and balance sheet don't address other matters of concern to you. You need to create your own key indicators to measure your success in quality, market share, or customer satisfaction.

If you are puzzled by what the numbers say, find experienced guidance to help you make the analysis. Sometimes your accountant can help; otherwise, a consultant who has run a company in your industry or a group of other CEOs or people experienced in business may help you see something you can't (or don't want to) see.

SHARING FINANCIAL INFORMATION WITH EMPLOYEES

As a business leader, you'll inevitably face the question of whether to share information about company finances with your employees and how much. Progressive managers make it a priority to educate staff on company finances. They make budgets widely accessible, at least within the confines of company facilities.

Still, it scares many managers—even progressive ones—to be open with the financial statements. As a rule, many people feel uneasy sharing money matters under any circumstances, considering them wholly personal. Moreover, many companies operate in such competitive fields that they risk a great deal if they bandy about their financial information.

Although I certainly advocate sharing financial and other key indicator data with employees, I don't think it makes sense to give them financial statements. Financial statements are documents meant for investors and accountants. Instead, what employees need is data relevant to their jobs. They also need to have this data analyzed in terms of the trends so that they can see how their work is impacting the company's prosperity.

Share numbers with your employees that will initiate clear action, and prepare and present a short, written analysis of those numbers. It is vital that each employee see a connection between not only his or her job but also each individual action and your financials. This will impress on each employee the fact that in business, virtually every action has a financial impact.

Many owners and managers are experts at product costs but ignorant of everyday, nonspecific business costs. You can hire consultants or professional staff to study your costs of labor, capital, and the rest, but you still need a basic approach to these issues. Furthermore, you have to know how to judge the results of their work.

Financial realities sometimes conflict with your vision and mission statements. When this happens, you may have to acknowledge the limits of quantitative analysis. Look to your business plan and vision and mission statements for guidance in making cost analyses.

TOOLS FOR UNDERSTANDING THE NUMBERS

To complete the exercises and worksheets in this section, you'll need:

- Your income statement and balance sheet.
- A list of accounts payable.
- A list of accounts receivable.

You may need to gather other data as well. The worksheets and formulas that flow from this information will help you compare projections to actual sales and expenses through your fiscal year, analyze cash flow, calculate and analyze various financial ratios, and determine key financial indicators and other information critical to owners, managers, and employees.

Put together, the worksheets and exercises provide you with useful financial tools and the framework for a monthly reporting package that will allow you to monitor your company's performance from many different perspectives and take some appropriate actions.

The worksheets in this section that will help you get a handle on understanding the numbers for your company are:

- Year-at-a-glance income statement.

- Year-at-a-glance balance sheet.

- Year-at-a-glance financial analysis.

- Budget variance report.

- Same month last year variance report.

- Analysis of cash position.

- Key financial indicators.

- Financial report to employees.

The following measures will help you to determine where you should be satisfied with your financial reporting:

- Do you have good cash management?

- Do you have timely and accurate financial data to review?

- Does the data you have help you make decisions? Do you need more? Do you look at all the data you receive each month?

- Is your company performing well compared to industry standards?

- Do you meet with employees at least once a month to review variances and trends?

YEAR-AT-A-GLANCE INCOME STATEMENT

Financial reports done by your accountants are useful for comparing this year to last year, but they don't tell you whether there is a big variation from projection and which month the variation may have occurred. If there is a large variation in one month, the year-to-date numbers are off the rest of the year after that point.

The income statement tells you how well your company has done over a period of time. It shows both revenue and expenses and arrives at a net income number at the bottom of the page.

Worksheet 3.1 on pages 88–89 synthesizes a number of important numbers into one form and on just one page. It offers a visual way to look at everything at once, which helps you think about business activities over the course of a whole year. Large variances should become quickly apparent.

Making It Happen

Using Worksheet 3.1, I find myself better prepared to ask pointed questions about budget items. I can compare them to other items, even other budget variances, and research important deviances from what I expected.

Some of these items may result from miscoding and similar technical problems, however, rather than expenses being much different than expected, but even glitches become easier to detect when the numbers run alongside one another.

Enter actual sales and expense numbers each month throughout the year. Calculate the monthly average column by taking the number of months so far this year and dividing by that number. This tells you if your monthly average is over your original budget and whether your current month is above or below average.

Reality Check

Consider these questions about your completed worksheet:

- Are your expenses what you expected, or are there large variations?

- Does each month look comparable, or are there large differences month to month?

- Do particular items seem out of line with the others in the report?

- Can you see trends that run across your business functions?

- Are there certain budget items that make sense compared against one another? For example, an increase in direct mail expense, followed in a month by a spike in revenue. What do those comparisons mean about your business functions?

Worksheet 3.1
Year-at-a-Glance Income Statement

	Month												Total	Monthly Average
	1	2	3	4	5	6	7	8	9	10	11	12		
Sales														
Cost of Goods Sold														
Beginning inventory														
Materials purchased														
Salaries & wages														
Production supplies														
Temporary help														
Shipping supplies														
Mailing & shipping														
Less ending inventory														
Total Costs of Goods Sold														
Gross Profit														
Sales & Marketing Expenses														
Salaries														
Sales commissions														
Direct mail														
Advertising														
Publicity														
Consulting														
Other sales & marketing expenses														
Total Sales & Marketing Expense														
Overhead Expenses														
Personnel														
Salaries														
Bonuses														
Payroll taxes														
Group life & health insurance														
Workers compensation insurance														

Employee benefit plans																		
Officers' salaries																		
Employment expense																		
Training																		
Temporary help																		
Total Personnel																		
Facilities																		
Rents																		
Property tax																		
Repairs & maintenance																		
Utilities																		
Property & liability insurance																		
Total Facilities																		
Administration																		
Accounting services																		
Automobiles																		
Bank charges																		
Computer supplies																		
Charitable contributions																		
Depreciation & amortization																		
Dues & subscriptions																		
Legal services																		
Licenses																		
Miscellaneous																		
Office supplies																		
Other professional services																		
Telephone																		
Travel																		
Total Administration																		
Total Overhead Expenses																		
Income (before taxes)																		
Income Taxes																		
Net Income																		

YEAR-AT-A-GLANCE BALANCE SHEET

Worksheet 3.2 illustrates items in your balance sheet in a format for easy analysis, month to month. It's a statement of what the company owns at a fixed point in time. It remains important to look at changes occurring from month to month because there is a direct relationship between changes in balance sheet and cash flow.

The Year-at-a-Glance Balance Sheet allows you to track balance sheet accounts for trends. It also allows a measurement system to track goals you may have to decrease inventory or decrease accounts receivable (both of which would increase cash).

The most important accounts to focus on are cash, accounts receivable, inventory, fixed assets, and accounts payable. More obscure accounts such as *other assets* generally don't change much month to month, so you don't need to focus on them. This format allows you to see important changes if they occur.

More aggressive owners and managers pay close attention to accounts receivable and payable on this worksheet. Accounts receivable and payable affect cash flow in mercilessly direct ways:

- If accounts receivable goes up, cash goes down.
- If inventory goes up, cash goes down.
- If accounts payable goes down, cash goes down.
- If fixed assets go up, cash goes down.

Making It Happen

Find the following items from your monthly balance sheet and enter each month on the worksheet. You will usually find these items on the balance sheet categorized as current (usually one year or less) or long term.

Assets

Current Assets

Cash.

Accounts receivable—money owed to you by your customers.

Inventory—your product waiting to be sold, either at your location or at a store.

Worksheet 3.2
Year-at-a-Glance Balance Sheet

Month	1	2	3	4	5	6	7	8	9	10	11	12
Assets												
Cash												
Accounts receivable												
Inventory												
Prepaid expenses												
Other current assets												
Total Current Assets												
Fixed Assets												
Accumulated depreciation												
Net fixed assets												
Intangible assets												
Other assets												
Total Assets												
Liabilities												
Current portion long-term debt												
Notes payable												
Accounts payable												
Accrued liabilities												
Other current liabilities												
Total Current Liabilities												
Long term debt												
Other liabilities												
Total Liabilities												
Equity												
Common stock												
Paid in capital												
Retained earnings												
Total Equity												

Prepaid expenses—items such as insurance or taxes (e.g., an insurance premium is paid upfront for a whole year; this entry spreads it out over the policy period).

Other current assets—miscellaneous items such as rent deposits.

Fixed assets—real property, equipment, and leasehold improvements.

Accumulated Depreciation.

Net Fixed Assets.

Intangible Assets—good will, intellectual property (rights, trademarks, patents).

Liabilities

Current Liabilities (an amount you owe to someone else, generally to be paid within one year)

Notes payable.

Accounts payable.

Accrued liabilities.

Long-Term Debt

Equity

Retained earnings—the amount of net income the company has earned and kept since the first day of the business, less dividends to shareholders.

Reality Check

Consider these questions about your completed worksheet:

- Are your accounts receivable and accounts payable accounts up or down over the period?

- Are there sharp variations during certain peak periods or seasons?

- Is your cash consistently at a comfortable level for operating the business?

- What is the current trend in inventory levels?

- Has your company acquired fixed assets in accordance with capital budgets?

YEAR-AT-A-GLANCE FINANCIAL ANALYSIS

This exercise pulls together useful information from both the balance sheet and income statement and calculates some ratios to give you an idea of the financial health of the company and how it changes month to month. The ratios included here are generally computed for whole industries. It is useful to compare your numbers to your industry.

The balance sheet items are asset management related and tell you how well you are doing increasing the value of what you own. The income statement items are related to profitability and tell you how well you are doing in that area.

Worksheet 3.3, as with the other year-at-a-glance worksheets, gives you a quick indication of how things are changing over time. The problem with financial statements is that you can't tell whether things have gotten better this month or worse. These worksheets will let you know immediately if there is a sudden downturn or a trend in that direction so that you can take corrective action.

Making It Happen

Find the numbers for the first four categories from your income statement and enter them for the appropriate month. Also enter the number of people you currently employ. Divide sales by number of employees to get the number for the last category under the income statement, sales per employee.

Enter the numbers for the first three entries under the balance sheet column. The remainder of the categories are calculated as follows:

Sales. Take this item from your income statement.

Gross profit margin. This ratio is sales minus cost of goods sold divided by sales.

Pretax profit. Take this item from your income statement.

Cumulative net income. An aggregate of the monthly income figures listed for the year to date, this tells you how close you are to your projections for the year.

Number of employees. Take this item from your payroll projection worksheets.

Worksheet 3.3
Year-at-a-Glance Financial Analysis

	Month											
	1	2	3	4	5	6	7	8	9	10	11	12
Income Statement												
Sales												
Gross profit margin												
Pretax profit												
Cumulative net income												
Number of employees												
Sales per employee												
Balance Sheet												
Total current assets												
Total current liabilities												
Working capital												
Current ratio												
Sales to assets												
Return on assets												
Debt to equity												
Accounts receivable days												
Accounts payable days												
Inventory turnover (annual)												
Inventory turn days												

Sales per employee. This number divides sales figure by the number of people the company employs to generate that figure. This is a popular tool for determining a company's efficiency—though standards change dramatically by industry.

Total current assets. Take this item from the balance sheet.

Total current liabilities. Take this item from the balance sheet.

Working capital. The amount by which current assets exceed current liabilities.

Current ratio. A basic test of solvency, you obtain this number by dividing the current assets of your company by current liabilities.

Sales to assets. A measure of how aggressively the business pursues sales, this figure (total current assets divided by sales) helps analysts determine how much unrealized sales potential a company might have.

Return on assets. This figure (pretax profit divided by total assets) compares profit with the amount of assets used to earn that profit. Acceptable figures vary from industry to industry.

Debt to equity. This figure (total liabilities divided by net worth or shareholders' equity) relates the company's debt to the strength of the equity in the company by owners or stockholders.

Accounts receivable days. First, divide sales by accounts receivable to obtain accounts receivable turnover. Then, divide 365 by the turnover figure. The result (also called *collection period ratio*) indicates how many days others are taking to pay you.

Accounts payable days. First, divide cost of goods sold by accounts payable to obtain accounts payable turnover. Then, divide 365 by the turnover figure. The result indicates how many days you're taking to pay your bills. It also tells analysts about your company's liquidity.

Inventory turnover (annual). This figure (cost of goods sold divided by the inventory item from your balance sheet) provides an indicator of how many times a year your company turns over its entire inventory.

Inventory turn days. Obtained by dividing 365 by the annual inventory turnover figure, this figure gives you a time period to compare directly with the accounts receivable and payable numbers listed previously.

This worksheet will be very valuable when you're dealing with potential lenders or investors. In this context, financial analysts sometimes ask for ratios not included on this worksheet. Some of the most important include:

Current liabilities/inventory. Obtained by dividing current liabilities by the value of current inventory, this figure tells managers how much the company relies on funds yet to be obtained from unsold inventories to meet its debt obligations.

Net sales/working capital. By measuring the number of times working capital turns over annually in relation to net sales, this ratio provides information about whether the business relies too heavily on credit to maintain its sales effort.

Return on investment. This figure prorates net profit by an individual investment vehicle's percentage of a company's total capitalization. It tells investors how soon they will recoup their money; it tells managers what form investments should take (limited partnerships, preferred or common stock, etc.).

Current liabilities/net worth. Considered by some lenders the most important test of a company's solvency, this figure indicates the amount due creditors within a year as a percentage of the investment in the business by owners or stockholders.

Reality Check

Consider these questions about your completed worksheet:

- Which numbers are trended in a positive direction and which in a negative direction? Are your ratios in line with industry averages?

- Which ratios concern you most? Are these issues that require immediate solutions (e.g., the current ratio) or long-term solutions (e.g., sales per employee)?

- Is the overall financial condition of the company getting better or worse?

- Can unusual or negative trends be explained satisfactorily?

- Are there other ratios that are particularly important to your business that should be included?

BUDGET VARIANCE REPORT

Managers go through all the effort of making a budget each year, but unless they compare their actual financial picture to what they budgeted, doing the budget remains a meaningless exercise. Budget variance is a wake-up call for managers to make midcourse corrections and to replan for the remainder of the year. With any variance, a manager should investigate what's gone right or wrong and hold people accountable for their spending.

Worksheet 3.4 gives an easy way to compare actual numbers each month to budget numbers, both for that month and the year-to-date (cumulative for the whole year). This worksheet is also useful for employee meetings and board of directors meetings.

Making It Happen

Enter your budget numbers for each item for the current month. Then enter the actual numbers that correspond to each category. In the third column, take the difference between the two (actual minus plan), and enter it in the $ variance column. For expense items, a negative number means you're under budget and a positive number means you spent more than you expected. Last, calculate the percent variance by dividing the $ variance by the plan $. A negative $ variance will result in a negative percent variance. Complete the whole exercise again for year-to-date numbers.

Notice that all the reports in this section have the same categories in the same order as the original budget. This makes comparisons between budget and actual much easier.

Reality Check

Consider these questions about your completed worksheet:

- Are there variances from budget of 10 percent or more (and/or $1,000 or more)? What accounts for these?
- If these variances are in the year-to-date column, are they also in the current month, or did they take place in a prior month?

Worksheet 3.4
Budget Variance Report

	Month-to-Date				Year-to-Date			
	Plan ($)	Actual ($)	($) Variance	(%) Variance	Plan ($)	Actual ($)	($) Variance	(%) Variance
Sales								
Cost of Goods Sold								
Beginning inventory								
Materials purchased								
Salaries & wages								
Production supplies								
Temporary help								
Shipping supplies								
Mailing & shipping								
Less ending inventory								
Total Cost of Goods Sold								
Gross Profit (Sales – Total cost of goods sold)								
Gross Profit % (Gross profit/Sales)								
Sales & Marketing Expenses								
Salaries								
Sales commissions								
Direct mail								
Advertising								
Publicity								
Consulting								
Other sales & marketing expenses								
Total Sales & Marketing Expenses								
Overhead Expenses								
Personnel								
Salaries								
Bonuses								
Payroll taxes								
Group life & health insurance								
Workers compensation insurance								

Employee benefit plans							
Officers' salaries							
Employment expense							
Training							
Temporary help							
Total Personnel							
Facilities							
Rents							
Property tax							
Repairs & maintenance							
Utilities							
Property & liability insurance							
Total Facilities							
Administration							
Accounting services							
Automobiles							
Bank charges							
Computer supplies							
Charitable contributions							
Depreciation & amortization							
Dues & subscriptions							
Interest expense							
Legal services							
Licenses							
Miscellaneous							
Office supplies							
Other professional services							
Telephone							
Travel							
Total Administration							
Total Overhead Expenses							
Income (before taxes)							
Income taxes							
Net Income							

- Are variances in cost of goods sold influencing your gross profit margin?

- Are your variances in the areas most companies find difficult to control: sales, marketing, and personnel?

- If the variance is negative, can you make immediate changes in your operations that will reduce the variance from budget?

- If the variance is positive, are you spending enough to support (what is probably) the increase in sales? Do you expect this increase in sales to continue?

SAME MONTH LAST YEAR VARIANCE REPORT

Budgets can be wildly above or below actual performance. Unforeseen factors can change the business a company does in a given time period. Projections—even good ones—are always suspect. However, last year's actual numbers are real, and it's important to take them into account.

This exercise allows comparison between individual months this year with the same months last year. This comparison allows for cyclical trends and historical perspective that many managers use as a basis for forecasting. It's important to compare your current numbers to prior years, especially when you're trying to grow a company. At publicly traded companies, stockholders always want to see if the company is doing better than last year.

Making It Happen

For the same month last year, enter your sales and expense numbers on Worksheet 3.5. Then use the same numbers from the Budget Variance Worksheet (3.4) to fill in the second column for the current month. Subtract last year from this year, and divide that number by last year to get the percent difference. A positive percentage indicates an increase from last year to this year. Do the same calculations again with year-to-date numbers.

Reality Check

Consider these questions about your completed worksheet:

- If the variance is great, again, do some investigation into what changed from last year.

- Are there variances that are greater than 10 percent? If so, can you explain them in a way that makes sense?

- Are your expenses up in any one category more than another?

- If the variance comes in the year-to-date column, in what month did it begin to occur?

- Are you prepared for any cyclicality you see with adequate cash?

Worksheet 3.5
Same Month Last Year Variance Report

	Month-to-Date			Year-to-Date		
	Last Year ($)	This Year ($)	Difference (%)	Last Year ($)	This Year ($)	Difference (%)
Sales						
Cost of Goods Sold						
Beginning inventory						
Materials purchased						
Salaries & wages						
Production supplies						
Temporary help						
Shipping supplies						
Mailing & shipping						
Less ending inventory						
Total Cost of Goods Sold						
Gross Profit (Sales − Total cost of goods sold)						
Gross Profit % (Gross profit/Sales)						
Sales & Marketing Expenses						
Salaries						
Sales commissions						
Direct mail						
Advertising						
Publicity						
Consulting						
Other sales & marketing expenses						
Total Sales & Marketing Expenses						
Overhead Expenses						
Personnel						
Salaries						
Bonuses						
Payroll taxes						
Group life & health insurance						
Workers compensation insurance						
Employee benefit plans						
Officers' salaries						
Employment expense						
Training						
Temporary help						
Total Personnel						

Worksheet 3.5 (Continued)

	Month-to-Date			Year-to-Date		
	Last Year ($)	This Year ($)	Difference (%)	Last Year ($)	This Year ($)	Difference (%)
Facilities						
Rents						
Property tax						
Repairs & maintenance						
Utilities						
Property & liability insurance						
Total Facilities						
Administration						
Accounting services						
Automobiles						
Bank charges						
Computer supplies						
Charitable contributions						
Depreciation & amortization						
Dues & subscriptions						
Interest expense						
Legal services						
Licenses						
Miscellaneous						
Office supplies						
Other professional services						
Telephone						
Travel						
Total Administration						
Total Overhead Expenses						
Income (before taxes)						
Income taxes						
Net Income						

ANALYSIS OF CASH POSITION

Worksheet 3.6 shows where money went besides paying for the expenses itemized in the income statement. A company made money but doesn't have cash to show for it. Why? Where did the cash go, how much was used by the operations, and how much was consumed by other things, such as asset purchases or paying down debt? This worksheet will analyze where the company's cash comes from and where it goes.

Worksheet 3.6 is a variation of the accountant's statement of changes in cash, which is a required part of a publicly traded company's financial reporting.

Making It Happen

There are three areas of cash use shown in this worksheet:

1. *Cash used for operations.* Cash flows from operating activities are generally the cash impact of changes in working capital accounts and from the basic operations of the company. Examples of increases to cash include net income, collection of accounts receivable, decreases in inventory, and depreciation. Examples of decreases to cash include a net loss, increases in accounts receivable balances, increases in inventory, and payments of accounts payable.

2. *Cash used for investing activities* (buying fixed assets, making acquisitions).

3. *Cash used for financing activities* (repayment of bank debt, long-term leases).

Enter the numbers for both the current month and year to date from your income statement (first line only) and balance sheet (remainder of the worksheet), and total the numbers in the shaded boxes to find net increase or decrease in cash for the period.

This is a complex worksheet. You may wish to get assistance from your CPA, especially if you have sales and fixed asset changes during the period.

Worksheet 3.6
Analysis of Cash Position

	Current Month ($)	Year-to-Date ($)
Operating Activities		
Net income (Loss)		
Adjustments to reconcile net income/Loss to cash		
Depreciation & amortization		
Changes in Assets & Liabilities		
(Increase) Decrease in accounts receivable		
(Increase) Decrease in inventory		
(Increase) Decrease in prepaid expenses		
(Increase) Decrease in other current assets		
(Increase) Decrease in accounts payable		
(Increase) Decrease in current portion long-term debt		
(Increase) Decrease in accrued liabilities		
Total Adjustments		
Net Cash Provided by (Used for) Operating Activities		
Investing Activities		
Additions to fixed assets		
(Increase) Decrease in other assets		
Other		
Net Cash Provided by (Used for) Investing Activities		
Financing Activities		
Line of credit borrowings (repayments)		
Principal payments on long-term debt		
Net Cash Provided by (Used for) Financing Activities		
Net Increase (Decrease) in Cash for the Period		
Cash at Beginning of Period		
Cash at End of Period		

Reality Check

Consider these questions about your completed worksheet:

- Was there a net increase or decrease to your cash for the period? For the year?

- Was the change from operational factors, investing factors, or financing factors?

- Are there changes you can make to positively influence your cash position?

- Is the company generating positive cash flow from operations?

- If the company is losing money, how is that loss being financed? With new equity? With payables?

KEY FINANCIAL INDICATORS

Worksheet 3.7 provides a one-page comparison of all of the key financial numbers comparing two years past to the current year. Used well, it will give managers a broad view, over three years, of trends in their business that relate to cash. For example, when I was running my company, I used this sheet at board meetings and with employees to illustrate, in simple terms, how the company was doing. It is a communications tool for displaying analysis I've done in other worksheets and exercises.

You may also find you need to develop key indicators that are particular to your business that may be more operational than financial. Examples include the number of projects completed, number of clients, profit as percentage of sales, returns for the month, employee turnover, and number of customer complaints.

Making It Happen

Keep a running total on all major financial numbers—cash, revenue, expenses, and income—and enter the current month when available. Record accounts receivable and accounts payable days, as well as total accounts receivable.

Reality Check

Consider these questions about your completed worksheet:

- Are the long-term trends (three completed years) what you want them to be?

- Have expense increases outpaced revenue increases?

- Are accounts receivable days and accounts payable days increasing or decreasing?

- Are overdue accounts receivable increasing or decreasing?

- Does this worksheet accurately display the financial strengths and weaknesses that your company has?

Worksheet 3.7
Key Financial Indicators

	Month											
	1	2	3	4	5	6	7	8	9	10	11	12
Cash												
This year–Projected												
This year–Actual												
Last year–Actual												
Two years ago–Actual												
Revenue												
This year–Projected												
This year–Actual												
Last year–Actual												
Two years ago–Actual												
Expenses												
This year–Projected												
This year–Actual												
Last year–Actual												
Two years ago–Actual												
Income Year-to-Date												
This year–Projected												
This year–Actual												
Last year–Actual												
Two years ago–Actual												
Accounts Receivable Days												
This year												
Last year												
Two years ago												

Accounts Payable Days

This year												
Last year												
Two years ago												

Accounts Receivable

Current												
30+												
60+												
90+												
120+												
Total												

FINANCIAL REPORT TO EMPLOYEES

Worksheet 3.8—also a communications tool—provides a simple way to keep employees informed about key indicators on which they can have an impact and help keep the company financially healthy.

Consider sending this worksheet and its attachments to all employees every month. In addition, have a monthly meeting to go over these numbers and answer questions about what they mean and how they relate to each job done in the company.

Making It Happen

Enter the numbers from the Key Financial Indicators Worksheet (3.7) for the current month as well as a running total for the year to date. You can then provide a simple analysis at the bottom of the page by determining which of the key items is up or down and translating the importance of these items for your employees. Attach the important financial worksheets developed in this section.

Reality Check

Consider these questions about your completed worksheet:

- Are you on target for where you expected to be at this point in the year?

- Are there things employees can do to help your company reach its financial goals and projections?

- Do employees understand the numbers and concepts presented in this worksheet? If not, how long will it take to teach them the things they need to know?

- Are you celebrating good news and acknowledging the effect of the hard work of particular employees?

- Do you ask the employees responsible for the changes you see to provide the explanation to the rest of the employees?

Worksheet 3.8
Financial Report to Employees

	Current Month	Prior Month	Two Months Ago	Year-to-Date
Sales				
Expenses				
Cost of goods sold				
Gross profit margin				
Sales expense				
Administration				
Total Expense				
Income (Sales – Expenses)				
Cash				
Inventory $				
Accounts receivable days (how long it takes people to pay our invoices)				
Accounts payable days (how long it takes us to pay our bills)				
Inventory turn days (how long it would take to use up the inventory we have on hand right now without adding to it)				

Attachments:
1. Year-at-a-Glance Income Statement
   Sales were (above/below) projections by _____ %
   Expenses were (over/under) budget by _____ %. Especially over budget were the following items:

2. Key Financial Indicators
   Profits were (above/below) projections by _____ %

3. Analysis of Cash Position
   Our cash was (under/over) projections by _____ %

WHAT'S NEXT

In the next part, we switch from measuring the results to driving the business. Your ability to increase revenue in a way that is profitable is key to making your business work. It is also essential to be able to turn first-time sales into long-term customer relationships or face the prospect of spending all of your time in the selling process.

PART III

BUILD LONG-TERM GROWTH

4

MASTERING THE ART OF THE SALE

Always bear in mind that your own resolution to succeed is more important than any other one thing.

—Abraham Lincoln

In some ways, sales and customer service are simple and direct, but their very simplicity is what makes them difficult because they offer no margin for error. That is, a sale either happens or falls through.

If marketing is mostly theory, selling is mostly action. Selling is one-to-one contact with the customer—talking, listening, and taking the order. Customer service is about getting another order.

Some CEOs come from sales backgrounds and love the showmanship and one-to-one contact. Other CEOs find sales a challenge and take every rejection personally. Whether you have a sales or other background, your company must constantly and aggressively sell its product. It must follow every lead to new prospects and new customers and meet new needs for existing customers. The CEO is the company's number one salesperson, and, as with everything else, what the CEO focuses on gets done. Sales must always be a primary focus.

SALES AND PROFITABILITY

Obviously, sales must be profitable or nothing else matters. Before you analyze any other aspect of your business, determine the profitability of your products and your customers. You can't set up appropriate sales efforts or sales compensation programs if you don't.

In general, 80 percent of your sales profits will come from 20 percent of your customers. Try listing last year's top 25 highest dollar-volume customers. Determine what they buy from you and how much money you take in per unit. Then, looking at your costs for these products, determine which customers bring in—not the most revenue—but the most *profits* to your business.

Sometimes your biggest customers negotiate such good deals (because they can) that profits are severely eroded. Similarly, your smallest customers can be the most costly because they don't buy enough goods to justify the cost of servicing the account. Don't be afraid to "fire" your least profitable customers by raising prices.

Once you ensure that your sales are profitable, the next step is to get to know your best customers. Your goal is twofold: You want to make existing customers' experiences with your company better to retain and increase their patronage, and you want to recruit more loyal customers like them.

CUSTOMER FOCUS

Whomever and wherever they are, your customers can get just about anything they want any time they want it. They can purchase products or services they need from you or from someone else, usually on the terms they want. Consumers have grown accustomed to getting better products faster and with a high quality of customer service. In fact, products are generally sold on one or more of three criteria—quality, value (more useful concept than cost), and service.

COMMITMENT TO QUALITY AND SERVICE

Austin-based Whole Foods Market is one company whose constant focus on quality and service has paid off. It is the market leader in natural foods retailing with sales three times greater over the past 12 months than its next competitor. The company's oft-quoted measures of success include customer satisfaction, team member excellence and happiness, return on capital investment, improvement in the state of the environment, and community support.

Whole Foods Market describes customers as, "our most important stakeholders in our business and the lifeblood of our business." The more than 20-year-old company—known for selling the highest quality natural and organic products available—operates 150 stores under 6 different names and employs more than 27,000 workers throughout the United States. Each store has a distinct personality and purchasing strategy designed to match the community it serves.

After an initial training, each new team member becomes part of the "buddy system" and is partnered with a veteran employee for additional one-on-one training and mentoring. Over time, individuals looking for promotional opportunities within the store can take mini-courses on leadership. To emphasize the value of each employee, company policy states that no one person can earn more than 14 times the average employee's salary, including the CEO. Policy limits the cash compensation paid in any one year to any officer to 14 times the average salary of all full-time team members. Team members are eligible for gain sharing based on four-week sales cycles. Teams also meet every four weeks to discuss problems and opportunities for increased sales.

Whole Foods Market has pursued an aggressive acquisition strategy over the past five years and hopes to increase its number of stores to approximately 300 by 2010. The company's commitment to customer satisfaction, team member excellence, return on capital investment, and community involvement are at the root of its success.

WHO ARE YOUR CUSTOMERS?

To determine who your top 25 customers are, you might ask what they have in common. Discover whether they're businesses or individuals and if they fall into a particular geographic area, income bracket, gender, or age category. Finally, you should ask whether they buy more from your competitors or from you.

A simple but very effective way to get an idea about what your customers think about your industry and your product is with *focus groups*. You can attract customers or potential customers to your focus groups by using small amounts of cash or product samples as inducements. Interview them and describe your product or service—or, better yet, show them—and ask for feedback. You then watch and listen to their reactions.

It's important to review the results of focus groups with as many managers as feasible. This educates your staff about the problems the product will face and gives your company the chance to respond. Staff needs to hear customers talking about what they want; it arouses their attention and makes innovation more likely.

You might also set up phone, mail, or in-person interviews with targeted customers. Send out written surveys to larger groups of customers or potential customers. Ask them to describe their responses in some detail.

Here are some specific things to look for in a focus group or survey:

• Find out how customers rate quality, value, and service in relation to your product.

• Look for information about price ranges and barriers, format or style preferences, service requirements, probable buying patterns.

• Find out how customers perceive your competition and how your customers get information about competitors and their products—advertising, direct mail, or word of mouth.

When you analyze the responses, focus on the features your product should have and what would make it more attractive. Determine where you outperform or lag your competition. Illustrate your results in graphic form and publicize them in your company. Let coworkers know what customers think of their work and what customers look for in the future.

Customer research also seeks to learn what motivates people to buy what you sell. In this process, anything that tracks sales in a detailed way helps you—this is why big retailers offer their own credit cards, encourage catalog orders, code their register receipts, and solicit web site registration. It's also the reason that direct mail marketers offer free items.

In summary, you can't control marketplace forces, but you can minimize your marketing risks. When you own a reliable base of data about your customers and their tendencies, you can sell selectively to people most likely to buy a particular product. If you know that middle-aged Philadelphia men buy red ties in February, you may know all you need to know to effectively use your marketing and sales budget.

QUALITY SALES

Studies of consumer and corporate buying habits consistently reinforce the notion that great service is key to quality sales. In some markets, customers rate service more highly than quality in choosing one product over another. *Market research* is an important tool for determining how well you serve your customers. However, your customers' needs and expectations constantly change, no matter what industry you're in. As a result, how often do you overpromise and underdeliver?

Make sure your market research helps your company by collecting information and adapting this knowledge to your changing markets. Do the following to make the most of your market research:

- Identify and define customer expectations concerning service.

- Translate expectations into clear, deliverable service features.

- Arrange efficient, responsive, and integrated service delivery systems and structures.

- Monitor and control service quality and performance.

- Provide quick, cost-effective responses to customers' needs.

Marketing's primary role is to create sales opportunities. If, for example, you enhance your product's usefulness to your customer by offering valuable benefits from a related line, you create an interested listener ready to learn more about your products. Each time you propose an innovative approach to a real need, you create a sales opportunity. To do these things, your sales force must know exactly how customers use your products.

THE RIGHT PERSON FOR THE JOB

Sales reps can be unpopular in an organization. They are often the bearers of bad news from customers. It's sometimes difficult to come to terms with the fact that your product may not be meeting all the customer's needs or that your competitors are producing a better product more cheaply than you are.

Make sure to pick the right people for these jobs—not everyone can do them. Salespeople thrive on contact with people, so make sure they have lots of contact with people inside and outside your organization. Expect some "us against them" problems, especially if you primarily pay salespeople on commission. A commission system makes salespeople very vulnerable to the performance of the rest of the company and can result in one group of employees "preventing" another from maximizing its income.

Salespeople are typically the most highly compensated employees, often earning more than the CEO. They also often receive trips and other perks for high performance. In my role as CEO, I found there was often jealousy between salespeople and other employees when it came to compensation and general attention. There was a constant need to reeducate employees about the risk and reward aspect of a salesperson's role. I found the best technique for minimizing problems was to pay attention and give credit to others in the company. Some salespeople understand this relationship and do it naturally; others need to be trained to appreciate what it's like for the rest of the staff.

Most sales are based equally on belief in a product and trust in the person selling it. People do business with people, not demographic surveys. Customers want—and need—to believe in what and from whom they buy. You have a great deal of control over shaping their beliefs.

CUSTOMER SERVICE PROFESSIONALS

It's an irony of business that your customers' perception of your company may be based on their contacts with some of your lowest paid employees: your customer service representatives. How these employees feel about you and your company can determine how your customers feel about *you*.

It's essential to set high standards for professionalism, etiquette, ethics, and positive attitude among your customer service reps. All of us have bad days, but having a bad day probably won't be a disaster in other areas of your company; in customer service, it will. As a business leader, you can make it easy and fun for your customer service reps to help your customers. For example, you might create quizzes to test employees on product information and other information that customer service reps are frequently asked; then award prizes and announce winners in the employee newsletter.

Most importantly, train everyone working with customers how to handle difficult situations. Keep good records about how many calls come in, the average time it takes to handle a call efficiently and completely, and common customer questions and issues. Also keep track of absenteeism and employee complaints.

Make sure that your computer programs provide easy access to virtually every aspect of product information. You should also set up programs that make it easy for your customer service reps to place orders and to track shipments and change information while customers are on the phone. Making it easy for your customer service reps will make it easy for your customers to use and enjoy your products and services.

SALES MANAGEMENT

Now that we've covered some of the basics about who's who in your sales and marketing effort, we turn to the topic of how you can manage and monitor sales. It's estimated that the average small company loses 20 percent of its customers each year. That means you should probably aim for 25 percent to 33 percent of each year's sales to come from new customers for your company to grow. Both new and existing sales are essential to the prosperity of your business: New sales bring increases to your top line and help grow your company, whereas sales from existing customers are generally the most profitable.

Keep meticulous track of all your sales and categorize them in different ways. For example, you might identify top products, what you sell, to whom you sell and what you sell them, where you sell, and what you sell profitably and what you don't. It's now possible to keep track of these statistics in real time, which allows you to keep better track of inventory. However, you still need to set aside time to determine what these numbers mean in terms of marketing and sales activities.

In addition, you should conduct monthly meetings, quarterly sales strategy planning retreats, and annual meetings with most of the management staff to discuss the implications of the sales numbers. Discuss changes you want to make to the product line as a whole from information you get from the sales figures. Use the annual meeting to identify customers you most want to retain and those that are not profitable.

At my company, we found the best way to discourage unprofitable customers was to raise prices. We often used the quarterly meetings to discuss the performance of the sales staff and their compensation. Sales compensation always raises an array of issues: whether you're paying too much or too little, whether enough or too little of the compensation is based on commission, and whether you're incentivizing your sales staff correctly to make the right kind of sales. We tried a variety of methods, some with better success than others, but always found we needed to tie compensation to profitability.

COMMUNICATING SALES DATA TO EMPLOYEES

Sales dollars are the customers' way of expressing appreciation for what your company does. It's important to share information about overall company sales by product line with all employees.

I believe it's your employees' right to know how they're performing; furthermore, they can often find ways to improve sales and profitability when they know the score. Company success is typically measured on sales volume or on sales volume increases. It's a point of pride for most employees to know and share their company's annual revenue. Whereas many employees don't understand profitability or are skeptical of its accurate measurement, sales volume is a number to which most can easily relate.

The goal of your sales and customer service programs is clear: Get the initial sale and keep the customer coming back for your product or service. Here are ways to ensure you meet this goal:

- Get and keep the best employees you can, employees who enjoy working with people and solving their problems, and who aren't easily deterred from their mission. Do your best to keep these employees happy and help educate other employees on their vital roles.

- Get out and meet your best customers yourself. Put yourself in the customers' shoes as often as possible and don't rationalize problems with your product or service.

- Learn to appreciate—and, when possible, act on—customer feedback.

- Celebrate sales increases with all employees. It's the goal of your company and a real opportunity for employees to take pride that the increase in sales represents their efforts to produce something of value for your customers.

TOOLS FOR MASTERING THE ART OF THE SALE

The worksheets and exercises at the end of this chapter will help you take a real look at your sales and measure your success in customer service. These worksheets include:

- Dollar sales month-to-month.
- Product sales by customer.
- Top-selling products.
- Sales by salesperson.
- Customer service key indicators.
- Customer service survey.
- Sales report to employees.

Work on your sales and customer service effort until you can answer yes to all of these questions:

- Are you satisfied with your revenue growth?

- Are all of your products profitable? Do you need to renegotiate with some of your customers?

- Can you identify customers or groups of customers whose business is not profitable for you?

- Are you satisfied with your plan to sell or deliver products via the Internet?

- Do you spend time with your salespeople, one-on-one?

- Do you spend time with your top customers, one-on-one?

- Are your sales and customer service people superstars?

- Have you asked for testimonials? Referrals?

- Are you maximizing the business potential from existing customers?

- Have you "fired" unprofitable customers by raising prices?

- Have you asked customers what they like about doing business with you and what they don't?

- Do you have a backup plan for the "what ifs"?

—What if sales were only 50 percent or less of forecasts?

—What if a major marketing effort fails?

—What if you lose your biggest customer?

—What if your competitors cut their prices?

—What if competitors come up with a new or better product or service than they currently sell?

DOLLAR SALES MONTH-TO-MONTH

Worksheet 4.1 is a simple and straightforward way to look at your actual month-to-month sales compared to projections by product. A great deal of information is contained in a very simple worksheet.

Better than an overall company sales summary, this worksheet enables you to identify:

- What is working and what isn't.
- Which product sales are steadily increasing.
- Which products need changes to remain viable.

Making It Happen

Worksheet 4.1 shows actual sales figures compared to sales projections by month and determines average sales by month. First, list all of your products or product lines in the left column. Take the projections developed in the Dollar Sales Projections by Product Worksheet (2.3), and add those in the second column. Next, on a monthly basis, add in your actual sales dollars by product.

If you have records of past years, use the worksheets to plot the numbers for these years as well. Add all sales by month and put that number in the second from last total column. Finally, divide this number by the total number of months for which you have sales figures (divide by 12 if you have numbers for the whole year) to get an average dollar sales figure by month.

Reality Check

Consider these questions about your completed worksheet:

- Do you see any cyclicality by product?
- Can you structure your sales and marketing efforts to take advantage of sales trends?

Worksheet 4.1
Dollar Sales Month-to-Month _____ (Month/Year)

Product	Goal for Current Month	Month												Total Year-to-Date Sales	Average Sales by Month*
		1	2	3	4	5	6	7	8	9	10	11	12		

*Divide total year-to-date sales by current month number.

- For which products are your goals greater than your actual sales?

- Is this because you were overly optimistic when making projections?

- For which products do actual sales exceed goals? Is this expected to continue, or is it due to a particular marketing effort?

PRODUCT SALES BY CUSTOMER

A goal of every company should be to sell as much of each type of product as possible to every customer it acquires. Worksheet 4.2 identifies dollars each customer spends with your company. Looking at three years' worth of data enables you to see whether customers are spending more or less on average than they did two years ago.

Because so much money is spent just letting potential customers know that you exist, additional sales to existing customers are very profitable business. Every company should have a plan to sell more products to existing customers. This worksheet can help you track whether your plan is working.

Making It Happen

Worksheet 4.2 helps you calculate dollar volume per customer over the past three years. Use the same three-year lists of products and total dollars per product you developed in the Dollar Sales Month-to-Month Worksheet (4.1) for the first two columns (A and B) of Worksheet 4.2. Add the total number of customers that buy each product for column C. Finally, divide column B numbers by column C numbers to get column D.

Reality Check

Consider these questions about your completed worksheet:

- Was this exercise difficult because so many customers buy more than one product or product type, or are your customers generally customers for one type of product only? (If you had a difficult time segregating customers by product, the total company numbers at the bottom of the page will be most meaningful for you.)

- Which products bring in the highest dollar volume per customer?

- In which products are the dollar volume per customer numbers going up each year?

- Are these increases because of price fluctuation, or has the number of units sold to each of these customers increased? (The shaded box in the bottom right of the worksheet becomes one of

Worksheet 4.2
Product Sales by Customer

Product	Two Years Ago			Last Year			This Year		
	Sales ($)	Number of Customers	$ per Customer (B/C)	Sales ($)	Number of Customers	$ per Customer (B/C)	Sales ($)	Number of Customers	$ per Customer (B/C)
A	B	C	D	B	C	D	B	C	D
Total Company									

your key indicators. Measured over time, this will tell you if you are increasing sales dollars per customer.)

- Is your customer base shrinking or increasing?

- Do a few customers account for a specific portion of a particular product's sales? If so, what can you do to take optimum advantage of that connection?

TOP-SELLING PRODUCTS

This exercise helps you determine which products sell the highest number of units and bring in the most revenue. If you have only one product, this will be easy. If you have more than one, it's important to know which products your customers like best. But even if you offer only five products, your top product is probably the one you should consider enhancing with add-on or similar products. You may also wish to analyze how you market these successful sellers and determine if you can make similar efforts with other products.

Making It Happen

Assemble a list of the sales in units and dollars of your products for the past two years. Rank them from top to bottom on Worksheet 4.3, starting with the product that sold the greatest dollar volume last year. Complete the worksheet by filling in the projected and actual units and dollars for the two-year period.

Reality Check

Consider these questions about your completed worksheet:

- For which products were your actual numbers above or below your projections? What caused the variances: the projections or your performance?

- For which products did your sales volume increase? Why?

- For which did it decrease? Why?

- Do the trends up or down in sales suggest long-term changes in your market? Or can they be explained by circumstances in your company?

- Are your top products related in any way? Could you create further products related to them? Can you market other products with them?

Worksheet 4.3
Top-Selling Products

Product	Last Year				This Year			
	Units		Dollars		Units		Dollars	
	Projected	Annual	Projected	Annual	Projected	Annual	Projected	Annual
Totals								

SALES BY SALESPERSON

Worksheet 4.4 helps you look at how well your salespeople are performing over time. It looks at sales both in terms of the individual salesperson and in terms of whether sales are to new customers or existing customers. You may choose to do separate worksheets per product or product group if you sell a variety of types of products.

This worksheet will allow you to compare the performance of salespeople and help you better coach or incentivize them to a different balance of new or existing customer sales.

Making It Happen

Compile a list of all salespeople in the left column. Next, add in projected and actual sales for this year. You may wish to do this each month using year-to-date figures, separating sales between those to new customers and those to existing customers. Repeat this exercise for last year. You may wish to use year-to-date figures in this area of the worksheet to have comparable data in both sections.

You can also perform the same analysis by looking at products that have been introduced over the past 12 months.

Reality Check

Consider these questions about your completed worksheet:

- Are some salespeople clearly outperforming others? Are some salespeople clearly underperforming when you know what is possible?

- Are you satisfied with the mix of new customers and existing customers?

- Is the performance of your salespeople increasing or decreasing over time? By each individual? For the group?

- Were your projections uniformly too optimistic?

- Is your sales compensation plan appropriate for the sales volume brought in for each salesperson?

- What percentage of total sales is brought in by each salesperson?

Worksheet 4.4
Sales by Salesperson

Name of Salesperson	This Year				Last Year			
	New Customers		Existing Customers		New Customers		Existing Customers	
	Projected ($)	Annual ($)	Projected ($)	Annual ($)	Projected ($)	Annual ($)	Projected ($)	Annual ($)

CUSTOMER SERVICE KEY INDICATORS

Worksheet 4.5 is a diagnostic tool that helps you monitor the workload and productivity of the customer service representatives and the department as a whole. Keeping the pulse of activity in customer service can provide a general indication of how well the company is performing. This worksheet and any other measurements of customer satisfaction are key to a general determination of operational efficiency. The worksheet can be used to track the productivity of the individuals who answer your telephones. Posting these measurements will give rise to the natural competition between individuals, especially for sales dollars.

Making It Happen

List each customer service representative by name and, if your telephone equipment and computer equipment allows, enter the number of calls each has answered, the percentage of time on the phone, the percentage of time each is not available to take calls, and the dollar volume of sales per sales rep. At the bottom of the worksheet, tally the number of calls by month in each category over the past two years.

The bottom half of this worksheet is a good indicator for sales; the more calls received, the higher the sales dollars for the month. If complaint calls have increased, it may be a measure of problems in shipping or in the quality of the product.

Reality Check

Consider these questions about your completed worksheet:

- Is the number of calls answered increasing or decreasing?
- Are order calls increasing faster than the number of calls in general?
- Are complaint calls increasing?
- How do the number of calls you receive relate to the various products you make or market sectors you serve?
- How do per-unit revenue or profitability numbers relate to customer service contacts?
- Can you find ways to reward super performers in terms of number of calls taken and sales volume?

Worksheet 4.5
Customer Service Key Indicators
For _____ (Month/Year)

Customer Service Representative	Calls Answered	Time on Phone (%)	Time Not Available (%)	Sales per Terminal ($)	Calls Answered	Time on Phone (%)	Time Not Available (%)	Sales per Terminal ($)

Totals

Last Year	1	2	3	4	5	6	7	8	9	10	11	12	Total
Calls Received													
Calls Answered													
Calls Abandoned (%)													
Average Talk Time													
Calls Categorized:													
Orders													
Inquiries													
Complaints													

Last Year	1	2	3	4	5	6	7	8	9	10	11	12	Total
Calls Received													
Calls Answered													
Calls Abandoned (%)													
Average Talk Time													
Calls Categorized:													
Orders													
Inquiries													
Complaints													

CUSTOMER SERVICE SURVEY

Worksheet 4.6 helps you look at how well your salespeople are performing over time. It looks at sales both in terms of the individual salesperson and in terms of whether sales are to new customers or existing customers. This survey assesses your customers' opinions of your products and services. Data gathered here can help improve your service to current customers. It may also help you get back customers you've lost or prevent the loss of other customers.

Making It Happen

Send this survey to each demographic group of customers. Try to send at least 50 surveys per group, if possible. You might select demographic groups by sales volume, product type, or particular distribution method.

You may get back only a small percentage of surveys sent. You can increase this response rate if you give customers an incentive to return it—perhaps a discount on their next order or a free premium. The larger the number returned, the better the data you will have from which to draw conclusions. You might consider encouraging customers to return the form directly to the company president by including a self-addressed, individually stamped envelope. You will get a better response and the responses will be more meaningful if customers believe the president of the company will read their survey comments. You can also conduct a survey by e-mail or at your web site, especially if you give an incentive to complete it.

Tabulate responses by taking each question individually, totaling the 1 to 10 score received, and dividing that number by the number of surveys received with that question answered. This will give you an average score for each question.

Distribute your scores throughout the company. A score of 8 to 10 means that you're doing a great job. A score of 5 to 7 means that you still have room for improvement. Finally, consider scores of 4 or under to mean you need to focus immediate attention on those areas of your company. Put together interdepartmental task forces to devise action plans to increase your levels of service.

Worksheet 4.6
Customer Service Survey

Please help us provide outstanding service by rating us in the following categories (10 = best).

Question	1–10	Comments
Telephone calls are answered promptly		
Customer service reps are helpful and knowledgeable		
Your orders are filled correctly		
You are informed about new products or product changes		
We are easy to do business with		
Items ordered are received in good condition		
Orders are received promptly		
We deal with problems efficiently and effectively		
Orders are complete and correct when received		
We offer good value for the price paid		
Products are easy to use		
Billing is accurate		
Credit terms are clear		
We provide timely responses to your requests		
What new products would you like to see us produce (include changes to our current product line)?		
What can we do to improve our relationship with you?		
Comments about other areas we missed in this survey:		

☐ There is more to say and I would like you to telephone me. The best time to call is _____ .

Name and Company Name (optional) _____

In addition, pay careful attention to the remarks in the comments sections. Call any customers who requested a response within a week of receiving their completed survey. Be sure to send a thank you message to all customers who provide their names at the bottom of the survey. This survey should be done annually and the results trended over time.

Reality Check

Consider these questions about your completed worksheet:

- Is customer service getting the priority it deserves in your company?

- Are most of your scores in the 8 to 10 range?

- Was there a similarity in customer comments, particularly by demographic groups?

- What can you do to immediately change customer perception for the better?

- Are your scores trending up or down over time?

SALES REPORT TO EMPLOYEES

Worksheet 4.7 is a communications tool that provides employees with a way to examine sales and receive a meaningful analysis of what the numbers mean. Circulate it once a month and discuss it at regular meetings. You can use this report as you would the Financial Report to Employees (Worksheet 3.8), and it gives you an opportunity to congratulate outstanding performers on the sales team and encourage everyone to get involved in sales and promotion.

Making It Happen

Complete Worksheet 4.7 with information from the Dollar Sales Month-to-Month Worksheet (4.1) and others in this section. Provide a simple analysis at the bottom of the page by determining which products are up or down from projections and translating the importance of these changes for your employees. Attach the important worksheets developed in this section.

Reality Check

Consider these questions about your completed worksheet:

- Are your sales meeting expectations for the company overall on a year-to-date basis?

- Are some products performing much better than expected? Why?

- Are some products lagging expectations?

- Are there reasons that can be corrected?

- What can each employee focus on to improve sales?

- Do employees understand the marketing concepts and numbers used in this report? If not, how long would it take them to learn enough to apply them?

Worksheet 4.7
Sales Report to Employees

Product	This Month		Year-to-Date	
	Projected ($)	Actual ($)	Projected ($)	Actual ($)
Total Company Sales				

Comments:

Products above projections:

Products below projections:

We were (above/below) projections for the month by ———%.

New accounts this month:

Attachments to this report: *Dollar Sales Month-to-Month.*

WHAT'S NEXT

Sales is the big driver of your business on the revenue side, but operations, the subject of the next chapter, is a big driver on the expense side. You must do both well to maximize profits. Next, we look at the reality of the consequences of how you produce your product and deliver it to your customers.

5

ACHIEVING QUALITY AND QUANTITY

Our main business is not to see what lies dimly at a distance, but to do what lies clearly at hand.

—Thomas Carlyle

The goal for operations is to achieve the highest possible efficiency, making the best use of equipment and human resources—in other words, to reduce costs without damaging sales. Therefore, operations is the natural choice to see to it that the business attains your goals for gross margin. Operations implementation entails looking at ways to constantly improve your process—to seek to make the time in production less and the quality higher. It means constant measuring and setting new standards.

SETTING THE RIGHT STANDARDS

Benchmarking is the art and science of setting a standard of performance by looking at what others in your industry do. It's straightforward and, when properly focused, highlights the important tasks that operations must accomplish. However, benchmarking doesn't automatically set the right goals. Would Federal Express have built its business with benchmarks tied to the performance of the U.S. Postal Service? It might have offered four-day delivery to beat the Postal Service by one day. Instead, it targeted a revolutionarily higher standard and gave us overnight delivery, forcing the Postal Service to measure itself against that (and setting a new benchmark).

The point is that market-based benchmarks—those pegged to the performance of your competitors—serve as minimum standards, not as the be-all and end-all. They work for starters, and only if you can't come up with better standards to measure your own performance. You do better to identify best-case performance standards and aim for those, irrespective of what your competition does.

It's easy to find performance standards for operations. How well your operations people meet deadlines measures time management. Actuals versus budgets measure cost control. Random sampling measures quality control.

In setting performance standards for operations, consider the following five items:

Five Critical Measures of Operational Performance

1. Customer satisfaction.

2. Productivity and efficiency.

3. Companywide (or total) quality.

4. Innovation.

5. Financial performance.

In operations, the fundamental objective of making money translates into production, inventory, and operational expense. Making money means keeping production high and inventory and expenses low.

Although operations is a greater focus in product-based companies, it is still important to service companies. Operational decisions are much more focused on people in service companies—such as the cost of salaries and benefits and unused time or unproductive time.

Defining Quality

The Malcolm Baldrige Quality Award has set the standard for defining quality for U.S. companies. The award was initiated in 1987 to make U.S.

companies more competitive in the world market. The seven categories in which companies are judged are:

1. Leadership.
2. Strategic planning.
3. Customer and market focus.
4. Measurement, analysis, and knowledge management.
5. Human resources focus.
6. Process management.
7. Business results.

Process management includes both processes that create value for customers, giving you a true competitive advantage, as well as those support processes that make sure you are running as efficiently and effectively as possible. The selection criteria looks at how companies did in these categories measured by an assumption that this is what it takes to be a quality-driven company: visionary leadership, customer-driven excellence, organizational and personal learning, valuing employees and partners, agility, focus on the future, managing for innovation, management by fact, social responsibility, focus on results and creating value, and a systems perspective.

Looking at these standards, notice that quality is no longer defined by looking at a single product output from a manufacturing line. Quality is inherent in the entire process from the first time a customer sees one of your brochures, through the first phone call to your salespeople, to a shipment to their location, and beyond. However, it doesn't stop there—quality also means meeting your customers' expectations that you will be there for them in the future when new technology brings new needs for them.

The Deming Approach to Quality

The inventor of Total Quality Management, W. Edwards Deming, began preaching his gospel of quality in Japan, where he went after World War II to help conduct a census. He had helped devise sampling techniques first used in the 1940 U.S. census, and in Japan Deming lectured to top

A HIGHER STANDARD

In mid-1999, the Air Transport Association, the trade group of America's major airlines, released a plan called "Customers First." The plan was the culmination of talks between the airlines, Congress, and the Department of Transportation regarding the lack of customer service among many of the airlines. Customer First was conceived to address this problem. Most U.S. airline companies have subsequently adopted the voluntary plan. It will be available to consumers via web sites and at airport ticketing areas.

The customer service reforms in this plan call for airlines to:

- Tell passengers about the lowest fares available.

- Notify customers of delays and cancellations as early as possible.

- Make a greater attempt to find passengers with lost luggage.

- Do a better job meeting passenger needs during long waits aboard an aircraft.

One of the first airlines to adopt these procedures was Dallas-based Southwest Airlines. In business since 1971, Southwest holds the airline industry's best cumulative consumer satisfaction record, a measurement kept and published by the Department of Transportation. Southwest's mission statement reads:

> The mission of Southwest Airlines is dedication to the highest quality of Customer Service delivered with a sense of warmth, friendliness, individual pride, and Company Spirit.

Southwest outlines its Customer Service Commitment to passengers in a 26-page booklet, which promises to share with its customer how it operates. It also say, "Foremost, we want you to know that it is *never* our wish to inconvenience our Customers. We tell our Employees we are in the Customer Service business—we just happen to provide airline transportation."

Southwest knows that situations will arise that aren't of its making such as weather delays, problems at terminals, and so on. But it also knows that Customers will look to Southwest to make sure these problems are minimized or that they result in minimal inconvenience. The airline has taken a proactive stance toward serving Customers, even when problems aren't their fault. They anticipate problems and have worked out solutions to be followed by their Employees before the unexpected happens.

business leaders on statistical quality control. He told the businessmen that Japan could dominate world markets if they stressed his definition of quality in their manufacturing operations.

Deming identified three phases of change that companies go through on the road to improved performance measurement systems:

1. Tinkering with the existing measurement system (e.g., the cost accounting system).

2. Cutting the "knot" between accounting and performance measurement.

3. Embracing change in strategies, actions, and measures.

Deming believed in online quality control rather than end-line control. To achieve it, analysts sample products during manufacture to determine the product's deviation from an accepted range of errors. As Deming saw it, any deviation is the result of one of two kinds of variables, either a special cause stemming from random events or a common cause arising from faults in the system. Deming argued that special causes account for only 6 percent of all variations and common causes account for 94 percent. In his view, most companies spend too much time trying to determine the nature of special causes rather than examining the system to find out what's behind the common causes.

Deming's analysis relies heavily on mathematics—a product of his background as a government statistician. However, anyone can understand Deming. One of his most simple underlying premises was that quality improves as variability decreases. To monitor variance, he advocated a statistical method of quality control. He argued that companies should strive for continuous improvement using statistical methods and analysis to maintain quality, instead of inspecting products en masse for defects once they have been manufactured.

Deming's work remained theoretical, but his many students have assembled a body of literature and consulting advice that gives the concepts a practical spin. His disciples identify 10 elements of total quality management. His statistical control theories may not apply to your operations, but you can use these points as a kind of diagnostic checklist.

On a day-to-day basis, which of the following things do you emphasize?

1. *Customer orientation.* Methods, processes, and procedures are designed to meet both internal and external customer expectations.

2. *Leadership.* Top management understands the quality process and supports the strategy through both words and deeds.

3. *Full employee participation.* Everyone in the organization is provided quality training. From top to bottom, everyone has the perspective, goals, and the necessary tools and techniques for improving quality.

4. *A sensible reward system.* There is a system in place that rewards quality to ensure continuous support for the overall effort.

5. *Reduced cycle time.* There is a strong effort to reduce the cycle times, in product or service output as well as support functions, following the maxim: "If it cannot be done any better, focus on doing it faster."

6. *Prevention, not detection.* Quality is designed into the product or service, so that errors are prevented from occurring rather than being detected and then corrected.

7. *Management by fact.* Managers use databased feedback to measure progress; intuition and gut feeling are put on the back burner.

8. *Long-range outlook.* There is a constant monitoring of the external environment to answer the question: What level of quality or service must we provide to customers over the next 12 to 36 months, and how can this goal be attained?

9. *Partnership development.* The organization promotes cooperation with vendors as well as customers, thus developing a network system that helps drive up quality and hold down costs.

10. *Public responsibility.* Corporate citizenship and responsibility are fostered by sharing quality-related information with other organizations and by working to reduce negative impacts on the community by eliminating product waste generation and product defects or recalls.

The lesson is that operations cannot be considered alone without looking at the interaction of all of the aspects of running a company.

ADDING NEW VALUE

A long tradition buttresses this thinking, but these days most managers with responsibility for operations spend their time doing three things—administering production, responding to crises, and improving performance. In other words, this means doing the job, putting out fires, and adding new value. However, experience suggests that we spend most of our time doing the first two and not enough time doing the third. On the contrary, we must do all three, and we need a great deal of information to bring it off, including data detailing what happens and why during the production cycle.

The just-in-time inventory control system popularized by Japanese manufacturers shows how this information can pay off. In traditional manufacturing, someone would deliver a big load of, for example, car bumpers to the people on the production line who installed them—more bumpers than the workers needed for the day's output. Most of the inventory would sit on racks off to one side, waiting to be used. The thinking here was that the company gained something by making one delivery of many bumpers. It did not consider the other side of the equation—namely, the cost of a fat inventory. It did not measure the benefit of the single delivery of bumpers against the cost of loading up with more than necessary.

Japanese managers were the first to make that measurement, inventing just-in-time inventory control and saving themselves a good deal of money in the 1950s and 1960s. They accomplished this by measuring, by gathering information about the production process, and asking what it meant. American managers followed suit in the 1970s, though it took them a while to overcome the biases of their traditional methods. For example, one management consultant tells of working as a summer intern at an appliance manufacturing plant in the Midwest. Detecting some inefficiencies in the plant's painting methods, he implemented a simple quality-control standard. He gathered data on the number of appliances that passed paint inspection and plotted a defect rate chart that he posted on a bulletin board. Workers had never seen their defect rate graphed before and were riveted by the charts. Their defect rate dropped from about 30 percent to about 5 percent.

Unfortunately, the story doesn't end there. After several weeks of improved performance, an upset operations supervisor tracked down the intern and asked about the charts. The intern, expecting praise, instead got a hot lecture about the problems he had caused down the line. Because the defect rate in the painting operation had dropped so dramatically, the company would have to lay off its rework people, who had no screwups to fix. The supervisor told the intern to take his charts off the bulletin board.

Information generates improvements, but not without cost. The intern's charts threatened the jobs of the rework people down the line—a bad outcome to the angry supervisor. However, that doesn't mean that you choose not to act on the information you gather, only that you know to expect that improvements of this sort will not always be welcomed immediately by the staff.

Critical thinking and the kind of innovation of the sort required to overcome the resistance to change are both key management duties.

WHAT YOUR INVENTORY TELLS YOU

To return to the idea of controlling the inventory, this makes a big target when operations sets out to improve your company's efficiency, but it presents managers with some hard questions. "It's good to think of inventory as a liquid force," says one New York-based consultant. "It pours around the decisions you make about your business. You can't make hard policies about how your inventory will be. The best you can do is have a few priorities and use inventory as a kind of ongoing barometer of what's going on in your business."

With service companies, *inventory* is people and the hours they are available to work with clients. Increasing efficiency leads managers to embrace nontraditional employment and compensation structures, including part-time or contract workers and flexible teams operating as so-called *virtual corporations.*

With manufacturing companies, some studies argue that you can reduce operating costs by more than 25 percent by managing inventory well. Things on shelves tie up cash; you spend money to make and maintain them—and then face the risk of damage or loss. Managers keep inventory as low as they can, at the risk of revenue-killing backlogs, spikes in supply costs, and production scheduling nightmares.

Leaving extra products on your shelves also tests the effectiveness of your marketing efforts. A quick walk through your warehouse, for example, tells you a great deal. Losing products accumulate, while winning products disappear; products that don't sell take up storage space that could go to faster movers. If your shelves groan under products that you expected to sell, ask your sales force and marketers why. Don't stockpile losers passively—which means don't ignore your inventory mix. You can cut inventory by 50 percent and still have piles of things in your warehouse that no one wants—in effect, you have a permanent inventory and an expensive one at that.

Some inventory problems have to do with the mix of products you stock, not with quantities. Retailers learn this the hard way. They balance the need to stay in stock against the need to turn inventory—a crucial measure of success in retailing. Most try to hit annual sales between 12 and 20 times inventory, which puts pressure on managers to keep only the best products in stock. A big mix of products makes their problems worse by lowering storage capacity for any single product, and retailers must remain open to buy—ready to purchase and stock hot items.

Managers in other businesses keep themselves open to buy by remaining flexible and market-responsive even when it means taking less of a profit than you want from one item to free up money and space for another. Growth also makes for complications in inventory control. You can't grow faster than you can deliver product to your customers. You may have to replenish inventory more often or stock more units of fewer products.

It's hard to quantify the connection, but some managers see inventory numbers as a reflection of accounts payable and receivable. Government contractors, for example, wait 60 days for payment, sometimes 90 days, and their accounts receivable run a deep negative. As a result, they rarely keep inventories larger than the value of their receivables minus payables. As a Maryland-based consultant to government contractors says, "You need to figure out where all the money has to go to make the business function and know what the timing has to be. If you're fronting a lot of money to payroll and product development, you're not (going to have much left for carrying) a big inventory. Make sure you can absorb the growth until it is paid for."

SUPPLIER CONCERNS

Another aspect of quality control is keeping a close eye on your suppliers. Over reliance on one supplier or source could be risky if it could suddenly not provide raw materials, inventory, or something else critical to your business. Get in the habit of monitoring with whom your company spends the most money each year as a supplier of critical materials. You may be on the list of this supplier's most important customers and represent a relationship they would like to expand. Take advantage of this.

You can—like some aggressive managers—tell suppliers that you know you spent $20,000 (or more) with them in the past year and that they might get more of your business if they're willing to negotiate on price discounts and/or terms. It is also a good practice to look at what you are spending with any given supplier for a whole year. We often don't realize what we spend in total when we receive monthly invoices. Taking a look at top suppliers also helped my company set limits for how much we wanted to spend in particular categories.

TOOLS FOR ACHIEVING QUALITY AND QUANTITY

In operations, as in financial matters, you can bring about a substantial improvement by using a series of basic analytic tools. The worksheets in this section provide the basics:

- Unit output by product.
- Units shipped.
- Average days to ship.
- Returns analysis.
- Backlog of orders.
- Inventory control report.
- Business partner (supplier) survey.

Ask yourself if you need improvement in your operations area:

- Do you self-audit your records and the maintenance of equipment?

- Are you reliant on only one supplier for a critical element of your business? Do you have backup plans in case that supplier goes out of business or is otherwise unable to supply what you need?

- If you have done business with the same supplier for three years or more, are you certain that it still produces the best value or the most state-of-the-art product?

- Do you have adequate internal quality controls, or are your customers the first to know if one of your processes failed?

- Are the facilities you use, which are adequate for today, also equipped for your growth plans?

- Do you have a working just-in-time inventory system?

- Are you making the best use of available new technologies in manufacturing?

- Are you tailoring new operations strategies for use on the Internet or for sales via e-commerce?

- Do you regularly chart and review operational performance?

- What is your biggest cost reduction opportunity?

- Have you adequately protected your intellectual property (with patents, trademarks, or copyrights)?

- Are your operations flexible enough to change when your customers' needs change?

- Can you manage the operational "what ifs" of the business?

  —What if a major source of supply were no longer available?

  —What if suppliers increase their prices on items important to your manufacturing?

  —What if you experience the loss of a lease, tools, or inventory?

  —Are your facilities and information systems prepared for a natural disaster or other physically destructive force?

UNIT OUTPUT BY PRODUCT

Worksheet 5.1 gives you a method by which to monitor production output by product for each month, year-to-date, and on average. You can use this worksheet to compare how many units you produce each month with how many units you sell of each product. It also allows you to see for which products you've increased production and for which you've decreased production (presumably because of increases or decreases in sales).

If output exceeds sales by a wide margin, you are increasing your inventory. If sales exceed output, you are using up inventory and run the risk of back orders over time.

The main benefit of doing this analysis is to post the numbers. This lets people know someone is paying attention to what they are doing. There is also the natural tendency of people to want to outdo themselves. Posting these numbers allows people to see their progress in increasing productivity.

Making It Happen

List each product you manufacture and, at the end of each month, enter the number of units produced. Keep a running tally of total year-to-date output in the first shaded column. Enter the average for the year in the last column.

Do this three times: once for last year, once to make projections for the current year, and once over the course of the year with actual numbers month-to-month. Last, enter the output numbers for the prior year at the bottom of the page.

Reality Check

Consider these questions about your completed worksheet:

- Is output on the rise for all products?
- Does output approximately match sales numbers?
- Is output up over last year?
- Are any of the trends indicative of factors that might affect production cycles in the coming year?
- How do unit-output figures compare with unit-revenue figures? In other words, which are your most cost-effective products?

Worksheet 5.1
Unit Output by Product

- ☐ Actuals Last Year
- ☐ Projections for This Year
- ☐ Actuals for This Year

Product	Month												Unit Output Year-to-Date	Average Unit Output by Month*
	1	2	3	4	5	6	7	8	9	10	11	12		

*Divide total year-to-date unit sales by current month number.

Total Unit Output Last Year

Month												Total
1	2	3	4	5	6	7	8	9	10	11	12	

UNITS SHIPPED

Worksheet 5.2 tracks the number of products shipped each week and each month.

Another way to get a feel for sales each month is to know how many units were shipped. Even taking into consideration the variety of prices charged for different products, if units shipped are up, sales probably are, too.

Units shipped is also a good gauge for determining whether to hire new production and fulfillment personnel. After using this form for a period of time, it is possible to determine how many units an average person can ship. If your totals get over this number, you may need to hire temporary help or even hire regular help for an ongoing need.

Making It Happen

List your products in the left-hand column. Track the number of units shipped each day for each of your products and enter the number once a week. At the end of the month, total the columns for each week in the total shipped column. Divide this total by four or five to determine the average number of units shipped per week. Enter this number in the last column. At the bottom of the worksheet, list units shipped in total for each month of the current year and the prior year.

Reality Check

Consider these questions about your completed worksheet:

- Are total units shipped up from last year?

- Is there a seasonality to your sales that means you have more units to be shipped at certain times of the year?

- How much of your weekly and/or monthly shipments were back orders? What's your current backlog?

- How do spikes in the units shipped figures alter your inventory control systems? Can you absorb some fluctuation? How much?

- Do these numbers seem to track with expectations based on sales figures for the same period of time?

Worksheet 5.2
Units Shipped
for —————— (Month/Year)

Product	Week 1	Week 2	Week 3	Week 4	Week 5	Total Units Shipped for the Month	Average Units Shipped per Week
Totals							

Items Shipped This Year

Month													
	1	2	3	4	5	6	7	8	9	10	11	12	Total

Items Shipped Last Year

Month													
	1	2	3	4	5	6	7	8	9	10	11	12	Total

AVERAGE DAYS TO SHIP

Worksheet 5.3 helps you determine how long your customers have to wait between the time they place an order and the time the product is sent to them. This worksheet will be most useful if you set a standard to meet. Use the average number of days to ship as a tracking for a service standard that you want to meet or beat.

Many companies try to ship off-the-shelf products within 24 or 48 hours of the order.

Worksheet 5.3
Average Days to Ship
for ——— (Month/Year)

Order Number	Order Date	Order Shipped Date	Days from Order to Ship

Total days from order to ship/Total number of orders = ——— Average days to ship

Making It Happen

Identify your orders (usually by order number) in the first column of Worksheet 5.3. For each order, enter the date the order was placed by the customer. In the third column, enter the date the order was actually shipped. Enter the number of days difference between the order date and the date shipped in the last column.

At the bottom of the worksheet, take the total number of days from the shaded box at the bottom right and divide by the number of orders you have listed in the first column. This number is the number of days on average between the time the customer placed the order and the time it was shipped.

Reality Check

Consider these questions about your completed worksheet:

- Is your current average number of days to ship an acceptable number to you? What is standard in your industry?

- What can your company do to decrease that number?

- Does seasonality or any other external factor influence turn-around time? If so, what can you do to anticipate this?

- Can you make a short turnaround time a stated goal for your company? Can you do this effectively?

- Again, how do these figures affect your inventory control?

- At what point does the time it takes you to ship an order start to interfere with sales?

- To what extent do different products require different turn-around times? Can you segregate shipping functions to handle these variations more efficiently?

RETURNS ANALYSIS

Worksheet 5.4 helps you determine how many of the units you send to customers are returned to you and why they are returned. It's a diagnostic tool.

As with many other worksheets in this section, it is important to track measures of productivity. If employees know you are paying attention to this measure, they will seek to improve the statistics themselves over time.

Making It Happen

List your products in the far left column of Worksheet 5.4. Then list the total quantity returned for each product in the second column. The third column has 10 separate sections. Each section has a reason for return code number that is explained to the right.

Enter the total quantity returned for each reason in this section. At the bottom of the columns, enter the total numbers for reasons 1 through 6 and reasons 7 through 10.

Reasons for return numbers 1 through 6 are errors on the part of the company. Use this worksheet to track these numbers, set goals, and decrease them over time.

On the bottom of the worksheet, enter the total units shipped. Calculate the percentage of shipments returned by dividing the total returns in the first shaded box by the total number of units shipped. Calculate the percentage of shipments returned for reasons 1 through 6 by dividing the second shaded box by the total number of units shipped.

Enter the number of shipments returned for reasons 1 through 6 for each month this year and last year.

Worksheet 5.4
Returns Analysis
for _____ (Month/Year)

Returns by Product

Product	Total Quantity Returned	Quantity Returned by Reason*									
		1	2	3	4	5	6	7	8	9	10
Totals:											

Total Returns for Codes 1–6 and Total Returns for Codes 7–10

Total Units Shipped (from Units Shipped Worksheet)	Shipments Returned (%)	Shipments Returned for Reasons 1–6 (%)

*Return Codes

1 = Product Not Ordered	2 = Shipment Received Damaged	3 = Wrong Product Received (order entry error)	4 = Wrong Product Received (shipping error)	5 = Product Defective
6 = Quality Not as Expected	7 = Ordered Too Much	8 = Customer Changed Mind about Product	9 = Exchange	10 = Other/Don't Know

Percentage of Shipments Returned for Reasons 1–6 This Year:

Month												
1	2	3	4	5	6	7	8	9	10	11	12	Total

Percentage of Shipments Returned for Reasons 1–6 Last Year:

Month												
1	2	3	4	5	6	7	8	9	10	11	12	Total

Reality Check

Consider these questions about your completed worksheet:

- Overall, are your returns increasing or decreasing?

- Is there any meaningful link between types of product and numbers of returns? Does this suggest anything for marketing or product development projects?

- Are many of the returns caused by problems on your end (reasons 1 through 6), or are they mostly due to customer needs changes?

- Do you think the number of returns could be lowered? If so, how?

Would returns be lower if customers better understood your product at the time they ordered?

BACKLOG OF ORDERS

Worksheet 5.5 helps you determine whether any orders have not been shipped by the end of the week (or other period of time that you choose). This is very important as a diagnostic monitor of production bottlenecks. A backlog occurs when an order is not shipped, which could be for a variety of reasons: The product may not be available, packaging may not be available, or shipping may be too busy to get it out.

Any items on this list should be investigated. The dollar volume column totaled on the bottom of the sheet will really focus your attention. Like excess inventory, backlog orders sap a company's productivity. Knowing this report will have to be made each week will usually prompt the shipping department to get all the orders out that it can.

Making It Happen

Worksheet 5.5 should be completed by shipping or customer service personnel every Friday. Any order not shipped by the end of the week should be documented by order number and customer name. Also entered should be the dollar volume of the order and the date the order was placed. The expected ship date and comments should indicate why the order was not shipped and when it will be. The total dollar volume of all the orders not shipped should be entered at the bottom of the worksheet.

Reality Check

Consider these questions about your completed worksheet:

- Are there orders backlogged every week or only occasionally?
- Are the reasons for backlogs usually the same?
- Are these problems that can be corrected? If so, how?
- How many of these orders will be canceled because of product unavailability?
- Has this problem gotten worse over time? With the same products?

Worksheet 5.5
Backlog of Orders
Week of _____

Order Number	Comments	Volume of Order ($)	Order Date	Expected Ship Date	Comments
	Total:				

INVENTORY CONTROL REPORT

Worksheet 5.6 helps you determine total inventory over a set time period and where inventory is inadequate to meet sales needs. This is another very important indicator of production bottlenecks.

Any items listed at the bottom of the page should be questioned. Asking the right questions at this stage could prevent these products from showing up on the backlog list later.

Making It Happen

In the first section of Worksheet 5.6, enter the total inventory numbers from the Year-at-a-Glance Financial Analysis Worksheet (3.3) for each month this year and last year. In the next section, list all products with less than two months' inventory at current sales levels, quantity currently on hand, and date that restocking is expected. This worksheet is an essential step in any move toward a just-in-time inventory management system.

Reality Check

Consider these questions about your completed worksheet:

- Is total inventory going up or down?

- Does inventory fluctuate in a cyclical or seasonal pattern? If so, can you use these patterns to manage inventory in the future?

- Does this increase or decrease fit with your cash management strategies?

- Will your restocking dates allow you to replenish your inventory supply before you run out of product?

What do inventory fluctuations suggest about your market sector? Your customers? Your internal operations?

Worksheet 5.6
Inventory Control Report
for _____ (Month/Year)

Total Inventory This Year

	Month											
1	2	3	4	5	6	7	8	9	10	11	12	Total

Total Inventory Last Year

	Month											
1	2	3	4	5	6	7	8	9	10	11	12	Total

Inventory at Low Level

List any items with under two months inventory on hand.

Product Description	Quantity Currently on Hand	Expected Restock Date

BUSINESS PARTNER (SUPPLIER) SURVEY

Worksheet 5.7 assesses how your suppliers feel about their relationship with your company. Using this data to improve your business relationships may lead to lowering your costs as well.

Making It Happen

You may get back only a small percentage of surveys sent. You can increase this response rate if you call ahead and tell your supplier contact to expect it or if you send the survey with an order. Try to specify a date by which you would like to have it returned. The larger the number returned, the better the data you have from which to draw conclusions. You might consider asking that the form be returned directly to the company president by including a self-addressed, stamped envelope. You will get a better response and the responses will be more meaningful if suppliers believe their survey comments will be read by the president of the company.

Tabulate responses by taking each question individually, totaling the 1 to 10 score received, and dividing that number by the number of surveys received with that question answered. This will give you an average score for each question.

Distribute your scores throughout the company. Congratulate yourself on scores of 8 to 10. Continue to improve on scores of 5 to 7. Consider scores of 4 or under to require immediate attention focused on those areas of your company. Put together interdepartmental task forces to devise action plans to increase your levels of service.

In particular, consider the remarks in the comments sections. Call any suppliers who requested it within a week of receiving their completed survey. Be sure to send a thank you message to all suppliers who provided their name at the bottom of the survey.

This survey should be done annually and results trended over time.

Worksheet 5.7
Business Partner (Supplier) Survey

Please help us improve our business relationship by rating us in the following categories (10 = best).

Question	1–10	Comments
Do you enjoy doing business with us?		
Do you feel we treat you as a vendor or as a business partner?		
Do our employees treat you courteously?		
Are you paid on time?		
Are we a larger or a smaller customer (10 = largest)?		
Do we supply you with enough information about our business for you to do your best work with us?		
Do we give you enough time to fill our orders?		
Could we make any changes in our business practices that would help us reduce your costs and result in lower prices for us?		
How could our relationship with you be changed to benefit us both?		
Other comments about areas we missed in this survey:		

☐   There is more to say and I would like you to telephone me. The best time to call is ——————.
Name and Company Name (optional) ——————

Reality Check

Consider these questions about your completed worksheet:

- Are you making it easy for suppliers to do business with your company?

- Are your employees creating partnerships with suppliers or treating them as vendors?

- What can you do to immediately change supplier perception for the better?

- Have suppliers told you anything that surprises you about the ethics of their communications with your employees?

- Are your scores trended up or down over time?

WHAT'S NEXT

Many managers begin their efforts at overall improvement with operations because they see the most money to be saved and the greatest improvement to product quality. Marketing, stimulating future growth, and generating new products are all crucial functions related to managing your operations, which is the subject of our next chapter.

6

GROWING PROFITABLY WITH MARKETING AND PRODUCT DEVELOPMENT

I have learned, that if one advances confidently in the direction of his dreams, and endeavors to love the life he has imagined, he will meet with success unexpected in common hours.

—Henry David Thoreau

G rowing a business means deepening your understanding of what drives the business, the market for your product or service, planning on the fly to take advantage of significant opportunities, and continuous product innovation. In addition, delivering better products faster and more efficiently to your customers requires a great deal of information. Marketing—in its broadest definition—is that information. It's a means of figuring out what works and doesn't work in attracting profitable customers for your business.

Few business factors challenge owners and managers more than marketing—perhaps because the term covers so many activities and disciplines. In many companies, marketing includes sales, customer research, and new product development. This confusion leads some managers away from giving marketing the attention it deserves.

Some companies boast that they are "market responsive" or "market driven," but in truth, in a world that depends on information, *all* companies must be market responsive. Your customers don't buy your products or those of your competitors for mysterious reasons; and whether you make hardware for cars, disk drives for computers, or movies for Hollywood, you must know who your customers are and what they want. You have to respond when their wants and needs change.

Marketing well may take more planning than any other area of your business, and most businesses have a specifically developed marketing plan. Marketing plans include not only an assessment of the world at large, but also activities you will undertake to impact that world and reach your customers. Your customers' perception is critical; your message to them about your product must be clear, have impact, and allow them to immediately see the benefit in buying your product.

Your marketing plan covers questions such as: How will you get that message out to them? What media will you use? How will you distribute your product? Furthermore, good marketing research often leads to new product development, answering questions about what else your customers expect for you to provide them and what risks there will be in launching a specific product.

This chapter takes you through the critical information for creating a marketing plan and covers the following topics:

- Determining your industry's potential and your competitors.

- Determining who your customers are and are not.

- Reviewing marketing activities to date.

- Looking at the development of new products.

- Looking at your industry.

To start planning your marketing efforts, first, you must consider how large or small your market is and who the other players are in that market. You learn much from the people in the marketplace who love your products and even more from those who don't. This means taking a hard look at your successes and your failures. It also means researching how well others are doing and analyzing that data to see what will be useful in your marketing efforts.

The details of your marketing plan will vary greatly depending on the industry. In publishing, for example, marketing entails huge expenses for advertising, publicity, and distribution because selling books or data relies on thousands of small and sometimes impulsive transactions. Marketing in the defense industry, on the other hand, entails meeting new customers face to face and networking on Capitol Hill and in the

Pentagon, because defense contracting relies on a few huge and lengthily considered transactions.

Industry information may also give you an idea of your market share. It may also tell you when developing new products may be most beneficial. Sources of industry information include trade associations, the U.S. Commerce Department, Standard & Poor's Industry Report, Dun & Bradstreet (many of these can be found in local libraries), annual reports of publicly held companies, online data services such as Lexis/Nexis and Dow Jones news services, and by talking to industry experts.

What you need to consider about the data on your competitors is whether this is an industry that offers opportunities for your company now and in the future. You also need to decide whether growth prospects are limited and, thus, if you should consider moving out of that market.

---

10 THINGS YOU SHOULD KNOW ABOUT YOUR INDUSTRY

1. What is the total buying power by number of potential customers and estimated dollar-buying volume?

2. Is this a mature or start-up industry?

3. What are the barriers to entering the industry?

4. Who are the industry leaders and why?

5. What is your position in your industry?

6. How many companies operate in this industry? Is the number increasing or decreasing?

7. Is there room for your company to expand its market in this industry?

8. Are there seasonal buying patterns in the industry?

9. Can you find projections of growth trends for the industry from trade groups, security analysts, or the federal government? How is the industry expected to change in the next year and in the next five years?

10. Are there factors that will affect the demand for products in the entire industry—technological innovation, government factors, or social or economic factors?

RESEARCH YOUR MARKET

It's easy to pose the questions you want to answer about your market and your competitors—and difficult to answer them. Managers must usually do more with less when looking outside the organization for factors influencing sales. Begin your market research by asking everyone in your company to write down everything they know about your competition and its products. From this, expect to pull a variety of impressions; your sales staff will probably have a perspective different from your technical people. In addition, order your competitors' products, call their salespeople, visit them at trade shows, and look at their web sites. Make a point of collecting and discussing this data at least annually. The object is to build a universe within which you can place and define your product and how your customers perceive you. You want to understand your competition so as to differentiate your product. The questions to answer include:

- What are the strengths and weaknesses of your competitors' products? Of their management teams?

- How do they mix quality, value, and service?

- Can you bring new products to market more quickly than your competitors?

CUSTOMER MARKETING DATA

In addition to researching your competition, you should also research your customers' buying patterns. Pinpoint what data you need and don't get bogged down in just having a lot of information. You need data from customers you have as well as customers you don't yet have, relevant to your particular product or service. That will be plenty to focus on.

Getting data is becoming much less difficult with the services available on the World Wide Web. It is possible to collect so much data on customers and their buying patterns that consumer groups have become alarmed and have tried to stop it. For most small businesses, the best sources of data are paying attention to your customers' comments and complaints. Really listen to how customers use the product and what would make it easier for them to buy and use in their setting. This data is available from your sales and customer service reps and can also be accessed directly through questionnaires and focus groups. This information is important to get for a new product in the design stage, the testing stage, and after the product is launched. Be creative by using your web site, contests, and discounts to get customers to provide information on your service, pricing, product quality, and their overall satisfaction with your company, personnel, and product.

Bear in mind that if customers offer solicited suggestions, they will become impatient to see solutions. Therefore, don't ask for information you don't plan to use. If you aren't intending to allocate resources to make customer service changes, don't ask customers' opinions on your service—you will just draw attention to the problem.

It's important to be discriminating when determining who your customers are and are not when preparing your marketing plan. According to one California-based marketing consultant, most companies use marketing information weakly and ineffectively. "Many businesses don't focus on who their real customers are because they are afraid to turn away business," she says. "It's important to identify who you don't want to sell to, so you don't squander your resources."

To do this, you need good trend information about your sales and customers. It is important to chart the information about sales and customers through time by week, month, or year; by product type; by location; by customer type; by marketing method; by dollar volume; and any other way that fits with your business.

THE MARKETING GAME PLAN

Jeffrey Schmidt and Clark Greenlee, who together started a successful espresso bar in the Country Club shopping district of Kansas City, had a clear eye on their market when they started out. Working as architects in Washington, D.C., they saw running an espresso bar as a good way to put their design skills to practical use. Coffee bars had proliferated in Washington, and Schmidt figured that Kansas City, his hometown, might prove a good market for a business relying heavily on atmosphere and inexpensive extravagance.

He and Greenlee did some basic market research. They went to espresso bars whenever they had the chance. They enrolled in Small Business Administration classes on starting a business and writing business plans. They contacted officials in Kansas City.

(continued)

Because Schmidt and Greenlee came to know their customer profile, they were able to use this information to open doors for their business even before they enacted any marketing efforts. For instance, other potential espresso bar owners had tried to get their plans approved by the large real estate holding company where the partners eventually opened their business. Schmidt and Greenlee stood out because their plan reflected their clear understanding of the market and their customer, forecasting sales and cash flow, and analyzing the Kansas City marketplace and the performance of analogous cafes and restaurants. This grasp of their customer also enabled Schmidt and Greenlee to secure a generous bank loan. As their bank officer said, "They had a great business plan, they came in and presented it very well and they seemed sharp and on the ball, qualities we look for in a borrower."

Latteland Espresso opened in spring 1993. By the end of the year, it had become one of the most thriving locations in the shopping plaza. Sales ran 50 percent ahead of projections, and the place turned a healthy profit. By the end of the decade, they had two locations in the city. In fact, their locations continue to do so well that Starbucks recently opened a store within a block of one of them. Sometimes your success inadvertently suggests a new market opportunity for your competition.

MARKETING ACTIVITIES

Sales are the best tool for measuring the effectiveness of your marketing activities, but they don't tell you everything you need to know. If sales increase, it probably means you're doing something right, but it sometimes takes some digging to find out what. You want to make the best and most effective use of your sales resources, and you need to analyze your numbers so that you know what "best" and "most effective" mean.

This includes looking for the highest margin. Find out what the average gross profit margin is for your industry and market, and see whether you expect to outdo or fall below the standard—and whether you can stay in business at that margin.

However, immediate profit isn't everything, especially when you undertake a long-term marketing program. Such a program might call for you to cultivate satisfied customers who believe they get their money's worth and will come back a second and third time. This may require you to sacrifice short-term profitability—a good sacrifice if you like your chances over the long term.

There are many ways to reach customers; the key is to know which way to reach the customers who will be interested in what you have to offer. Marketing activities include these and more:

- One-to-one sales.
- Direct mail.
- Personal phone calls.
- Brochures and catalogs.
- Classified ads.
- Yellow Pages.
- Newspaper display ads.
- Newspaper articles.
- Magazine ads.
- Magazine articles.
- Radio.
- Cable TV.
- Network TV.
- Web sites and Web ads.
- Billboards.
- Direct mail.
- Promotional items.
- Seminars.
- Demonstrations and contests.
- Trade shows/fairs.
- Catalogs.
- Telemarketing.

- Newsletters.
- Public relations.

Great effort will likely be spent, whatever activity or combination of activities you choose, on telling the customer about your product. Tell your customers how your product will enhance their lives, and show them your empathy for their exact situation.

In addition, know what you want to accomplish with a specific marketing activity: Do you want to increase awareness? Draw someone into your location? Have them call your sales office? Buy from your web site? Order from your catalog?

Be sure to give customers the right way to get in touch with you, and don't neglect to track your results meticulously. In the course of my business, I did a lot of direct mail. It was critical to know not only what worked and what didn't, but also when it worked—as in when the cash would come in from each effort.

PRODUCT DEVELOPMENT

How you define your product will have much influence on how you approach product development and marketing. If you think you sell cars, you might not think of yourself as the provider of a moving environment. You might think your customers are simply coming to buy a car, but what would they ask for if a car did not exist? They would want something that could comfortably, safely, and reasonably inexpensively move them from one place to another—anywhere, even difficult to reach locations. Defining your product by solving customer problems is essential.

Product development is the incremental process by which you make an idea into a product—and thereafter increase the product's quality and usefulness to your customer as time passes. Thus, product development has to do with existing products as well as with new; indeed, most companies develop their best new products from ones they already sell. They begin developing successor products the moment they think of the original.

Truly new products are rare, and no prudent manager waits for a brainstorm before making improvements to existing products.

However you get to the new product, the generation of new ideas is the most interesting part of product development. In many ways, it's the most creative work of the company—and as many people as reasonably can should take part.

SOURCES OF INNOVATION

The sources of innovation at your disposal include your employees as well as your customers. Innovations often come from routine customer comments. The company that translates the wishes of its customers into products appealing to a broad market succeeds almost automatically.

When new ideas emerge, help employees do preliminary research by considering these questions, especially about competition:

- Is this product one that could be sold easily along with other products we currently sell?

- Does it have a large market potential?

- Would this product be costly to produce?

- Does it have direct competition? Could you produce a superior product?

- How did this idea originate? From an existing product? From a gap in the market? From an unresolved customer need?

- Does the origin of the idea say anything about *other* new products you might consider?

Successful products also come from looking at what's hot in your industry or at what your competitors do better than you do. This requires keeping tabs on your competitors. Stay on the mailing lists for competitors' products and read trade journals with an eye to developments that signal new needs in your marketplace.

It's important to pursue new products even if your current lines sell well. The best kind of product development extends the interest in your products to new audiences while retaining the old.

Your marketing and sales departments should welcome new products because they offer something new to talk about to customers who may have bought existing products for years. They can rekindle interest in your entire product line.

As technology develops, it becomes more and more difficult to stay on the cutting edge in any given industry. Managers must make decisions about where their technical strengths lie, invest there, and purchase other knowledge. How you define what you do should be clearly tied in with your company's *core competency*. Your core competency is the thing that you do best. It is the strongest of your strengths. In my company's case, it was taking complex data and translating it into something simple to understand and simple to use.

The Nordstrom department store's core competency is in developing a relationship with customers. Accordingly, they define their product as the service their sales associates add to the value of merchandise with this philosophy:

Offer the customer the best possible service, selection, quality, and value.

Much of product development stems from knowing your core competencies. Historically, approximately 90 percent of a company's proprietary products or technology came from in-house development and 10 percent outside. In the future, the breakdown may become 50–50, and the definition of "outside" may come to mean contract work, joint ventures, university research, and consultants.

All this drives up costs, making product development not only the most creative but perhaps the riskiest function inside the organization. Managers must forecast how well new products will do and know when to make changes. They must also know when to abandon a project.

ASSESSING COSTS AND RISKS

New products are high-risk ventures, challenging you to anticipate and minimize the risks you undertake. The following chart assesses the riskiness of a particular new product:

	Existing Customers	New Customers
Existing products	Lowest risk	Some risk
New products	Some risk	Highest risk

Smart managers expand their product line incrementally, moving in small steps from product to product and market to market. As they go along, they ask themselves key questions:

- Does the product come from a need you know your customers have? Or do you merely think it's a need? What's the evidence of that need?

- If specific customers want the new product more than others, can you bring them into the development process? Would they pick up some of the development costs? Would they commission the product outright?

- Will this new product fundamentally change your internal operations? If you have inventory under tight control, will this product interfere with that discipline?

- Are you counting on the quality of the product—not just value or level of service—to sell the product? If one of these three factors weighs more heavily than the others, which does?

- How many competing new products are in the market already? If interest centers on a competitor's product, is there room for you?

MINIMIZING RISK

People in product development turn an old advertising joke on themselves: "I know half of my development money is wasted. I just don't know which half."

You minimize the loss of that money if you know the following:

- You must maintain high quality with the new product.

- Customers familiar with your existing products must find the new one easy to use.

- Target customers must think the product has been made just for them.

- The product must add value to your operations without adding much new cost.

If product development is a central activity in your company, give it an equal footing with marketing, sales, operations, and finance in the planning and implementation process. In this way, product development not only supports the core business plan but also helps to define it.

LAGGING YOUR MARKET

Through the 1980s, Mead Corporation's Lexis®, a computer-based legal research service, dominated its field. Lexis was one of the first sophisticated and widely used online services, and it made a fortune for Mead, kicking more than $50 million a year up to corporate headquarters on revenues of around $400 million. In the midst of all this promise and money, Mead decided to milk the Lexis subsidiary rather than cultivate it.

However, the company invested little money in developing or improving Lexis services. As a result, other data providers entered the market. By the early 1990s, Lexis was only one of many legal online services and it lost market share fast. In 1994, Lexis was sold and their new parent company made other strategic acquisitions of legal content providers to help them regain some of their previous market share. "Technology and the marketplace passed them," says a former Mead manager. "Senior management was content to remain a broker of public-domain information while competitors were developing value-added services. They paid the price."

The lesson is that if you decide to create a new product, you must also make the commitment to maintain it in the long term. Remember that a new product that succeeds won't remain alone for long—keep the momentum going by making it a priority.

MARKETING GOALS

However you monitor its effectiveness, your marketing department should seek to remove the barriers blocking communication between you and your customers. This usually takes the form of research and information gathering, but whatever form it takes, it needs to focus on two objectives: simplicity and sales.

Your marketing goals should seek to:

- Increase the number of potential customers who come into contact with you.

- Increase your conversion rate, so that more of these potential customers actually buy from you.

- Make sure they buy again.

- Use this information for product improvements and the development of new products.

Doing marketing well depends on your ability to pursue new ideas through the ordinary course of business. Small companies tend to fare best here because, being small, they remain nimble. Big or small, however, companies do poorly when turf battles erupt or factions create unwritten rules that resist change. To get around this, managers create cross-functional teams to foster product development, calling on people from finance, marketing, and operations to work together on a single new product. This can cause some confusion, but the creative upside is well worth the risk.

TOOLS FOR MARKETING AND PRODUCT DEVELOPMENT

Like operations, marketing brings a particular perspective—and particular priorities—to management. The following worksheets and exercises will help you make the most of your opportunities:

- Assessment of competition.

- Product sales by marketing method.

- Product development checklist.

Ask yourself these questions about your marketing and product development effort:

- What is your biggest competitive advantage?

- Do you, as a group, clearly understand your customers and markets?

- Do you know where you are positioned in your market?

- Are you regularly creating the next generation of new products and services and offering them to existing customers?

- Is overall customer input (positive or negative) trending up or down?

- Are your products and services out of date?

- Are you losing market share?

- Is your pricing appropriate and competitive?

- How do you decide when to initiate a price change?

- Could a competitor put you out of business?

- Could a government or technology change put you out of business?

- What is the biggest threat to the long-term survival of your business?

ASSESSMENT OF COMPETITION

Worksheet 6.1 provides a means to keep track of competitors' progress in the market and to learn from their successes and failures. Being able to anticipate how a competitor will act or react can provide a significant advantage in planning your strategy.

Keeping track of your competition is more important as a sales tool than as a means of setting goals for product development or service. It is important to know what they do well because your customers will know, even if you don't.

Making It Happen

List all the major competitors you know about. Use industry magazines, trade association contacts, financial reports, or news services to make sure you have a complete list. Some entrepreneurs even telephone competitors directly to discreetly inquire about their sales volume, products, and pricing policies.

Obtain their catalogs or other marketing materials, and buy their products or use their services. Ask friends what they like and don't like about the competitors' products.

After reviewing publicly available data on competitors, prepare this detailed assessment of the competition. This assessment will help identify competitors' strengths and weaknesses in products, quality, service, and price.

Reality Check

Consider these questions about your completed worksheet:

- Can you counter each competitor's weaknesses with strengths in your product or service? How else can you turn their weaknesses to your advantage?
- Could they counter your weaknesses with their strengths?
- What parts of the market is your competition moving into? Moving away from? Do these trends have any bearing on your business?

Worksheet 6.1
Assessment of Competition

Competitors Name and Location(s)

Parent Company Information

Product Lines

Estimated Market Share

Year	Sales	Net Income	Total Assets	Owner's Equity

Rate the following areas in order to determine major strengths and weaknesses of the competitor. Check the box to rate each area as a Strength (S) or Weakness (W).

	S	W	Comments

Briefly describe the competitor's reputation, competitive advantages and disadvantages, and overall marketing strategy:

- Are your competitors more stable and better capitalized than you are? Does this matter much in your market?

- How does your company's market position compare to those of your competitors? Are you a market leader or a market follower? Is there an advantage to being one or the other (which is more profitable over time)?

PRODUCT SALES BY MARKETING METHOD

Marketing a product often costs more than the manufacture of the product itself. Ineffective marketing efforts result in failed products, even if the products themselves meet every other criterion for product success.

To spend marketing dollars most effectively, the company must know what works, spend its money on those activities, and seek to eliminate or modify efforts that are less successful. This is a constant process—a marketing method that has worked for years may decline, and another type of effort may suddenly become more important. To this end, it's important to track not only what the sales were by product but also which of the company's sales efforts made the customer aware of the product, decide to order it, and place an order by phone, mail, or in person, to the company directly, or through one of its other distribution channels.

Making It Happen

Most companies use a variety of marketing methods. Worksheet 6.2 lists many of these methods across the top. To begin, list your products and the total dollar volume sales attributed to each in the first and last columns on the sheet. Then determine how much of your business is new and how much is from customers who have done business with you before.

All of the new business should be broken down into how the customer first heard about you: by mail pieces you sent out, through the phone book, from telemarketing, from an advertisement (television, radio, or print media), through someone who sells for you (i.e., a retail establishment), through one of your sales reps, by word of mouth from another satisfied customer, or from some other channel. In the top left portion of the box, list the actual dollars attributed to that type of marketing. Once all the boxes are filled in, use the bottom right corner of the box to calculate the percentage of business attributed to that effort by dividing the total sales effort by the new sales total.

Reality Check

Consider these questions about your completed worksheet:

- Is one type of marketing responsible for most of your sales dollars? In total or just in one type of product?

Worksheet 6.2
Product Sales by Marketing Method for ——————— (Year)

Note: For each method, sales dollars are on top, and a percentage of the total sales is on the bottom.

Product	Direct Mail	Telephone Book	Telemarketing	Advertising	Distributors	Sales Force	Referrals	Other	A New Sales Total	B Repeat Business	C Total Sales (A + B)
	$	$	$	$	$	$	$	$	$	$	$
	%	%	%	%	%	%	%	%			

Method (column group header over Direct Mail through Other)

Total ($):

- Is this because your marketing expertise is limited or because you've tried other methods and this is the one that works?

- Are most methods of marketing represented to some extent, or are many boxes blank?

- Could you use other marketing methods that you aren't currently using?

- Is a disproportionate amount of your business either repeat or new? (You may be missing new opportunities if it is mostly repeat. However, if it is mostly new, it may mean that customers are not satisfied enough to return.)

- Does it say anything about new products you haven't considered?

- Why aren't you producing a requested product now? Is there little demand? Is it too difficult to begin the process?

- Who should follow up on ongoing communications?

PRODUCT DEVELOPMENT CHECKLIST

Even if product development is routine at your company, it is easy to realize at the last moment that some important step was missed—packaging not ordered, price discounts not set, no plan for notifying current customers, and many other common missing pieces that can undo an otherwise well-thought-out plan. Worksheet 6.3 helps you make sure you have covered all the important steps in the product development process.

Making It Happen

Once you have decided to pursue development of a product, there are many decisions to be made and things that must be done between idea and prototype. Worksheet 6.3 lists some of the many items. Chief among these are projected ship date and initial quantity. Experience is the best guide to make these decisions, but most small companies try to schedule twice the normal production time to new products and keep early batches to the smallest cost-effective unit.

Although production and operations usually require the most attention during new product development, don't ignore marketing efforts. Especially if the new product moves away from or beyond traditional markets, more time and effort will have to go into sales and promotion.

Some owners and managers fall into the trap of thinking that they can sell a product *after* they've made it. Try to keep the production and marketing functions as simultaneous as you can. This worksheet can help. Meet with your product development team regularly and review the checklist. Use it as a record of each step, and add to it items that are relevant to your company.

Reality Check

Consider these questions about your completed worksheet:

- Have you discussed the new product and its development with all employees who will play a role in the production, marketing, or sales of this product?

- Did you include their input to make this process as smooth as possible?

Worksheet 6.3
Product Development Checklist

Product		Initial Quantity
Projected Ship Date		
	Check All That Apply	Comments
Production		
Design Specification		
Materials Required		
Person-Hours Required		
Temporary Help Required		
Equipment Required		
Miscellaneous Production		
Storage Requirements		
Other Packaging		
Other Costs		
Licensing Fees		
Order Entry		
Pricing Discounts		
Shipping Schedule		
Distribution		
Marketing		
Marketing Research		
Marketing Plan		
Pricing		
Methods		
Stuffers		
Direct Mail		
Telemarketing		
Sales Reps		
Commissions Schedules		
Packaging with Other Products		
General		
Set Sales Goals		
Determine Costs		
Calculate Breakevens		

- Did you set a realistic timetable to get everything done?

- Will you have sales as soon as the new product is ready to ship? How do expected sales change the initial quantities you'll produce?

- Have internal production and operations functions gotten ahead of external sales and marketing functions? If so, what can you do to bring the two together?

WHAT'S NEXT

Now that you know how to bring your products to market and to grow your business, I turn in the final two chapters to leadership tactics for guiding your business and communicating your values. You'll learn how to manage your employees on a day-to-day and long-term basis and how to manage your own growth as a leader.

PART IV

LEAD WITH COURAGE

7

DRIVING EMPLOYEES TO PEAK PERFORMANCE

A people that values its privileges above its principles soon loses both.

—Dwight D. Eisenhower

The quality of human resource management in your company determines the success or failure of most of the other goals you have set for yourself. If you manage people well in all aspects—hiring, training, coaching, reviewing, compensating, motivating, promoting, and celebrating—the impossible often becomes possible.

The single biggest mistake made by CEOs and other managers is spending more time analyzing and acting on the company's financial particulars than on its people issues.

But you can't talk about employing people today without talking about the erosion of trust between employees and their bosses. A recent Watson Wyatt WorkUSA® survey showed that only 39 percent of employees trust the senior managers, and only 31 percent feel that their companies do a good job communicating with them.

Lack of trust is probably the biggest problem in corporate America today, and it can't be ignored at small companies either. How can you be sure your employees trust you and believe in your goals for the company? The simple answer is that you must be trustworthy.

Owners, CEOs, and managers must all behave in a way that inspires trust. If you talk to one employee about another in a negative way, that employee learns what he or she can expect from you. If you come in late and leave early, you send a message about acceptable behavior. If you aren't honest about critical issues, don't expect to find trusting employees when you need them.

SET THE STANDARDS FOR YOUR EMPLOYEES

Another significant finding of the Watson Wyatt survey was that only 52 percent of employees see the link between their company's business objectives and their jobs. This number was at 72 percent only two years before the survey. Increasingly, employees are feeling disconnected from their managers, their peers, and their jobs.

One result of this disconnection is the rise in fraud (by CEOs, boards, and managers) and in workplace violence (by employees). People who don't feel committed and connected to other people and their welfare act in ways that are callous, self-centered, and dangerous. Not recognizing early signs in your business can have catastrophic results. Just ask the ex-employees of Enron and Arthur Anderson. And as is so dramatically illustrated by these cases, disconnection and abuse takes place at all levels.

Setting standards for acceptable behavior at your company is as critical an area of focus as any other. And start at the top. Your own behavior as CEO sets the standard. We will cover that in detail in the next chapter.

Demand that all employees treat one another—not just customers—with respect. Encourage respect for deadlines and create a forum for listening to individual concerns. Create a culture that encourages employees to feel and express passion for their work and one that celebrates work done well.

In addition, be sure to recognize and promote employees who solve problems and help others solve problems. People who make things happen and who don't let anything prevent their pursuit of doing the right thing are precious to the success of your company. Make sure they know that you know who they are and fully appreciate their efforts.

INVEST IN PEOPLE

Think of the difference one person can make when that person is highly motivated to get something done; then think of a group of people, pulling together toward a common goal. A high-quality team of people working together is your single biggest competitive advantage. Don't assume that you pay employees to come to work and that ought to be enough.

Conduct monthly management staff meetings to review the employee data you'll compile using the worksheets in this section. Then evaluate management performance based on how well your managers implement the actions decided on in these meetings.

Look at your payroll as an investment. It's just as important to have a plan for your human resource dollars as for any of the money you spend on plant and materials.

Quality in Your Workforce

You have a right (and a duty) to select the right employees for your workplace. Don't give up that right. If your intuition tells you not to hire someone with all the right credentials on paper, don't hire them. While you can't (and shouldn't) discriminate based only on gender, ethnicity, and a number of other criteria, you can (and must) be discriminating in choosing people in terms of their skill, character, and ability to make a positive contribution.

List the character traits you want your employees to possess. While the exercise may be challenging, the rewards are profound. Consider questions such as: How important are initiative and resourcefulness? What about trustworthiness and loyalty? Getting this right is likely to prevent employee lawsuits later.

One of the most important characteristics of a superior workforce is that all employees remain employable. This means that you employ only those people whom your competitors would want to hire if they could. It should be a goal of your human resource planning to seek state-of-the-art employees. Employees should know that you expect excellence from them and that they probably will need to invest in themselves through outside training to keep their end of this bargain.

From the beginning, you should decide how many employees are optimal to do the work and what skills and qualities you want them to possess. You can look at the quantitative issues objectively by looking at overtime rates, the amount of temporary help needed, and the numbers of errors made and subjectively by the amount of stress you see in the workplace and what other employees tell you.

You may be able to readily identify the skills you need from new employees, but you can also do a more objective analysis by identifying the total skill set you want from your employee base. Find out what you already have by doing a skill-set inventory, and then hire for the qualities you find are still missing.

Hiring Right Is Key

Recruiting and hiring are often done in haste, leaving the company to repent in the long run. To counteract this tendency, set up your hiring process at a time when more rational heads prevail, and make it difficult, if not impossible, to hire unless the process is completed.

Today, there's a reason to be concerned about negligent hiring. *Negligent hiring* means you and your company can be sued if one of your hires injures other employees, especially if you could have foreseen a problem but did not do a thorough check of the new employee before hiring.

The following five essential hiring practices should always be used:

1. *Require outside testing.* Allow a competent, impartial professional interviewer to administer both paper and pencil and verbal tests. Professional testing firms can administer valid psychological tests for intelligence, stability, even determinations of addictive or dishonest personalities, as well as skills tests of important technical abilities in your workforce. I find testing often validates a suspicion I already had but wasn't yet ready to come to terms with.

2. *Conduct a rigorous personal interview.* This includes asking general attitude questions, how you would manage your boss questions, how you would manage your staff questions, questions relating to the applicant's understanding of the financial workings of a business and your department's role in the

business's overall success, questions relating to the applicant's ability to set goals and his or her expectations about achieving goals, questions relating to specific skills required for the job, and general communications required by the job.

3. *Arrange a peer group interview.* This part of the process encourages applicants to speak more freely and helps determine how comfortable they will be in working with their peers. Follow up with a meeting of everyone involved in the hiring decision to determine if there is a group consensus about the applicant's suitability for work at your company.

4. *Do a background check.* Don't neglect this, even if it is an employee's cousin or your competitor's best salesperson. It's very easy to set up an account with an investigative firm online and to relatively quickly and inexpensively find out if the applicant has a criminal record or a history of DMV problems, lawsuits involving previous employers, workers' compensation claims, and so forth.

5. *Do a reference check.* You can conduct these over the phone, but they may involve a request in writing. Reference checking is less effective than it used to be, although you may still find a few people who are willing to talk. Most former employers play it safe and verify only dates of employment and salary.

Finally, I recommend including a statement on the application that information given by the applicant must be true and that it will be checked. I immediately disqualify anyone who is dishonest about any information that is pertinent to the hiring decision—that includes fudging on job titles, years of service, and salary history.

EFFECTIVE COMMUNICATION

Productive and positive communication with an immediate supervisor, as well as with coworkers, is a make-or-break issue for most employees. As we all know, the business world necessitates both formal and informal communication. Formal communication flows from the supervisor and follows the policies and procedures in the company manual. Informal communications are those that flow from other employees about "the way things are really done around here." When these two sets of communications are out of balance, morale at your company will likely suffer.

Make your internal computer network a resource for every kind of data your employees need. Virtually all of the worksheets covered in this book can be filled in with your company's information and made available for employee reference. Your employee handbook should also be made available online. Surveys can be conducted completely via e-mail, and you can also make yourself accessible by e-mail for questions or comments. Performance review and other forms, as well as other human resource communications, can take place through an effective human resource information system (HRIS) designed for your size of company.

By no means should communication be conducted exclusively via computer. Always conduct employee orientations and performance reviews face to face. Create other avenues for informal, face-to-face feedback as well. Mark these appointments on your calendar so time won't slip by and opportunities won't be missed. Chats over morning coffee, celebration lunches, afternoon walks, and brown bag resource talks all are valuable opportunities for discussing issues or developing rapport.

REAL PARTICIPATION

The Virginia-based AES Corporation is the largest global power company in the world. Founded in 1981, the company has 158 facilities in 28 countries and employs approximately 36,000 people around the world. AES believes that every employee should participate in the strategic planning process, even in the design of his or her own workplace.

AES promotes adherence to four principles: integrity, fairness, fun, and social responsibility. The company conducts annual surveys of employees at individual locations and companywide to ensure that it's standing by these principles. The surveys are designed to determine whether employees follow the ethical principles both with other employees and with customers and suppliers.

Provide Regular Feedback

The idea of providing regular feedback is to let employees know how they are doing individually, in their departments, and as a part of the company as a whole. Feedback is often subjective by necessity, but it can be objective as well. The best kind of feedback is the kind employees seek out, not the kind that's forced on them.

You can take certain steps to maximize the effectiveness of the process of giving your employees feedback. For instance, if your intranet has easily available sales data, sales employees will look at it often and judge their need to change performance accordingly. In this manner, you can empower your employees to change their behavior on their own or ask for help before they are "graded." In addition, you can give employees copies of all of the evaluation materials that will be used during their employment (surveys, annual review forms, team feedback tools) at their orientation. By showing employees how they will be evaluated, you'll help them understand what is expected of them.

Review Performance

Managers are taught to conduct formal performance reviews annually, but it's a good idea to conduct additional, informal, mini-goal-checking sessions at least quarterly. Schedule these sessions when you will be fresh and when your mind won't be elsewhere. Conduct them off-site if that will help ensure you won't be distracted. If you put a lot of thought into the process upfront, your employees will do most of the preparation for the sessions themselves.

As a prelude to a review session, it's useful to ask employees for feedback about what is standing in the way of their progress. Many human resource professionals advocate asking employees to formally rate themselves and then compare their rating with their manager's rating during the formal session. I find this leads to a lot of anxiety and not much dialogue. If you ask people what is holding them back and what you can do to help, they will candidly explore their own weaknesses from a place where they are open to feedback.

During the review meeting, turn these areas for improvement into goals for the coming year. Ask the employee to consider ways to create goal statements with measurements by quarter. These goals then become topics for your quarterly reviews.

Many companies make use of team performance reviews in addition to the traditional manager's review. In these reviews, members of a peer group evaluate an employee. Although I see tremendous value in the concept, I have found that the average employees today are not ready to accept criticism from peers; they barely tolerate it from their supervisors. Peer reviews can create anger and resentment rather than increased learning, unless months of preparation precede the feedback. The best way to transition into this system is to make it available as a tool for self-evaluation to those individuals who seek promotions. If employees are open to learning about how they are perceived because they want to use this information to increase their opportunities, they will better be able to accept the negative messages.

Also plan to conduct regular manager reviews to evaluate managerial effectiveness. Employees need to know they will have the opportunity to speak candidly about their manager's behavior.

COMPENSATE FAIRLY AND WELL

Determining proper compensation is one of the most complex aspects of running a business. It's wise to seek outside assistance when designing a compensation program to ensure that it is fair and appropriate. A compensation professional will evaluate and compare the jobs in your organization to one another, as well as to similar positions on the open market, to determine a fair and competitive package. The compensation professional can also assist in devising the correct formula for incentive compensation, that is, bonuses for doing an outstanding job.

You don't want to overpay, but don't make the mistake of negotiating hard to underpay. It's not worth the time and expense you'll face when you need to replace high-quality employees who depart after a year or so because of subpar compensation.

Benefits form a significant portion of the compensation package. Regardless of the other benefits you may offer—retirement, vacation, and so forth—try to provide the best health insurance coverage you can. This is the benefit that makes the most difference to employees and their families in the short run.

MAKE TIME TO MANAGE

Companies schedule regular meetings for all sorts of other tasks. We can't expect improvement in our human resource issues unless we regularly devote time and attention to meeting these challenges.

An employee-ranking system is a simple tool managers can use to share their concerns about their department's employees. Managers can use a simple 1 to 10 rating scale, in which they assign 9s and 10s to superstars and 4s or below to employees who no longer belong in their current jobs—or perhaps even with your company. Managers can rate employees in a variety of categories and dimensions to reach a composite score. Some of these dimensions include character, communications skills, and technical abilities.

The intent of this process is not only to review employees, but also to hold managers accountable for constant improvement in the caliber of the personnel they hire. It's a way to get managers thinking about what they can do each month to create more 9s and 10s.

Manage the Managers

Between the tasks involved in recruiting and hiring and those involved in discipline and termination lie the continual assessment and improvement of your employees' knowledge, willingness, and action on the job. This brings us to the subject of employees who rank all the other employees—your management staff. Managers should rate 8 and above on a 1 to 10 employee rating system, or, if they are new, reach that rating within six months. There should be little flexibility with this decision. Managers who rate lower than 8 are not likely to possess the qualities you want as a model for the rest of the staff. Remember, a manager's key role is to coach great performance out of others.

Don't Tolerate Destructive Employees

We all make the mistake of keeping employees around long after they know and we know they are not right for the job. Some behaviors should never be tolerated in the workplace. They are toxic to your culture and will hurt your work environment immeasurably if not checked. They may seem harmless in small doses, but they can create a pattern of behavior that can ruin a company. Employees whose actions reveal lack of character and resulting unethical behavior should not be allowed to continue destroying the company.

You may think judging employees' ethics is inappropriate—that they should be judged on work performance alone. But whether you realize it or not, you set ethical standards for your company through many avenues, such as your own behavior, the rules in your employee handbook, the performance review process, the compensation system, and how and whom you promote. You also set standards by the behaviors you encourage and tolerate in your employees.

Studies confirm that the single biggest determinant of ethical behavior of employees is the behavior of top managers and their ability to communicate culture effectively. If top managers aren't willing to walk your talk, expect employees to follow suit.

FOUR THINGS YOU SHOULD NEVER TOLERATE FROM EMPLOYEES

1. *Gossip.* Rumors can be incredibly disruptive to a company. A lack of information can get rumors started, and frank explanations can usually stop them. However, some employees thrive on the admiration of others when they seem to be "in the know." Define gossip as clearly as you can and tell employees what you expect them to do when they hear it. First and foremost, that you don't repeat it. Along the same lines of gossip, remind employees that all e-mail sent or received on company computers is considered company business and not private correspondence.

2. *Violence or threatening or abusive behavior.* Termination should be immediate for any employee who engages in any form of violent or abusive behavior. Workplace violence includes threatened or actual abuse and can be verbal or physical. These behaviors only escalate with time and are never excusable. Any employees involved in workplace violence should leave the workplace immediately and be placed on a paid leave of

absence for a few days while you investigate the situation and consult with your attorney. Don't assume this couldn't happen in your company—it's estimated by the Occupational Safety and Health Administration (OSHA) that two million Americans are victims of workplace violence annually.

3. *Dishonesty and theft.* The term *theft* can include the theft of time, office supplies, and the use of office equipment for personal projects. Set standards for what is acceptable use of company assets. Security experts say as many as 30 percent of workers steal, resulting in an estimated loss of $50 billion a year from U.S. companies and contributing to as many as one-third of business bankruptcies.

As for dishonesty, I have a zero-tolerance approach. I dismissed members of my accounting staff for what may seem to be petty reasons: one for using $5 of petty cash as personal lunch money, another for telling me he was home sick when he was out of state on a long weekend vacation. If key staff members are not honest with you about small things, how can you be sure they will tell the truth "when it counts?"

4. *Substance abuse.* Substance abuse is more rampant than most employers know. The U.S. Department of Health and Human Services estimates that from 6 to 11 percent of adults are substance abusers. Substance abuse costs U.S. employers an estimated $100 billion a year. Call your attorney to make certain you follow the Americans with Disabilities Act (ADA) requirements. Illegal drugs are expensive and have led financially desperate employees to commit fraud. They have also been implicated in violent behavior in the workplace.

HUMAN RESOURCE ADMINISTRATION

Compliance with the myriad employment laws is essential to avoiding lawsuits, fines, and even criminal prosecution. There are so many laws and regulations that it takes a professional in this area to provide adequate protection for your business.

The administrative portion of the human resources function can often be done most cost effectively by outsourcing it to specialists. Outsourcing can be done effectively for writing and updating employee handbooks, designing compensation programs, administering employee surveys, administering benefits (including creating benefit statements), and providing training for many types of skills.

Employee handbooks are essential for companies with more than a dozen employees, and it's helpful to post the handbook on your intranet. Make sure the handbook reflects your culture and isn't a cold introduction of rules and procedures. Rules should only make work easier or create a cultural accountability; don't expect them to cover every situation. Our handbook always included expectations, not just rules. The handbook must be updated at least annually to keep legal requirements current. When a handbook is introduced or updated, it should be carefully explained at an employee-wide meeting. Drafting of new policies can and should be a highly participative process to allow employees the opportunity to think through the kind of behavior and expectations they want to have of one another. In addition, be sure that you are personally willing to live with each policy in your handbook.

One of the most important provisions of the handbook is that employment is "at will." Subject to various state laws, this means that your employment relationship with your employees is at your discretion; that is, you may fire them at any time except for reasons that are illegal. Specifically, state that employment can be terminated at any time without cause and that nothing in the handbook should be construed to be a contract of employment.

AVOIDING LAWSUITS

An ounce of prevention is certainly true when it comes to avoiding lawsuits, but despite best efforts, lawsuits can happen to any company. Keep focused on your business, and let the attorneys deal with lawsuits as much as possible. If you are in business for any length of time and have a number of employees, odds are that one or more of those employees is bound to sue you. In my nine years' experience running a company, many employees threatened suit, especially at the time of termination, but I had to pay to settle only one and none went to court.

MANAGING PEOPLE WELL

Here are some final tips for managing the human resources role:

- Give human resource matters the planning and time they deserve. Decide to treat employees fairly, but also commit to spending most of your time with employees who can grow to become outstanding members of your team. Spend as little time as possible with discipline problems, and help employees who need to leave do so in as gracious and honest a way as possible.

- Provide the best benefits you can, but remember, what your employees want most from you is free—the benefit of your wisdom and expertise to help them grow in their careers and your recognition of their accomplishments.

- Get the support you need to deal with people issues. Find other business professionals you trust and solicit their outside perspective to help you solve problems. Although you may be tempted to procrastinate, act quickly when you make decisions about people and get on with running your business. As I discuss in the next chapter, knowing when to ask for outside help is key to great leadership.

TOOLS FOR MANAGING AND MOTIVATING EMPLOYEES

The worksheets and exercises at the end of this chapter will help you drive employees to peak performance. They include the following:

- Performance review.
- Team feedback.
- Management skills feedback.
- Employee ranking system.
- Human resource key indicators.

How does your human resource program rate on the following questions?

- Do you spend enough time to be sure you are hiring for the long run?

- Do you have written policies as required? Are they updated at least annually?

- Are you certain you are in compliance with the basic HR standards, for example, employees versus independent contractors, exempt versus nonexempt employees?

- Are you following procedures that are most likely to keep you out of employee lawsuits?

- Have you set standards for performance and day-to-day behavior? Are the standards clearly communicated and followed?

- Does your compensation and benefit structure allow you to hire and retain highly talented employees?

- Are your employees overworked? Do you spend a large amount in overtime and temporary help? Is that figure increasing?

- Do you tolerate gossip or other behavior that undermines employee morale?

- Do you give enough feedback to employees about their performance? Do you review them individually at least annually?

- Do you insist your employees stay employable?

- Do you have a plan for the loss of any key employees?

PERFORMANCE REVIEWS

The performance review process should be done in two parts. Part A of Worksheet 7.1 is a feedback mechanism from the employee to the manager. It's important for the manager and employee to have a dialog over the issues, looking both at the employee's individual behavior and within the larger context of corporate culture.

It's important to find out upfront what the employee thinks leads to higher productivity within the company's culture and what results in obstacles to the employee's best work. It's vital to begin the process with an open mind, listening to the needs and problems the employee is willing to address.

The employee is much more likely to be forthcoming and identify his or her own inadequacies if the manager first allows discussion about inadequacies in the organization's support of the employee.

The second part of the performance review process is a subjective analysis on the part of the manager as to the various aspects of the employee's work performance. It covers the employee's specific job responsibilities, the quality and quantity of the work done, and how he or she interacts with others.

When you conduct this review, get away from the office or at least find a place you won't be disturbed. Do this both to complete the worksheet and, later, to meet with the employee. You should also set up criteria for each of the possible scores of 1 to 10 based on your own expectations of your entire employee group. When completing an individual's review worksheet, consider looking back at others you have done to help maintain consistency. Also, if you have reviewed this employee previously, look back to see which areas show improvement. In the comments section, list specific incidences to illustrate the employee's behavior.

Making It Happen

Give or e-mail the employee the first part of the performance review to complete about a month before his or her review date. Specify a date by which you expect to have the form returned. Set a date for your meeting when the employee returns the form. Give yourself a few days to read the employee's responses and consider thoughtfully how they compare

Worksheet 7.1
Performance Review
(Part A)

TO:

FROM:

It is time to schedule our annual performance review meeting sometime during the next month. Please fill out this form as completely as you can and return it to me by _____. It will help me to help you. We will schedule a time to meet as soon as possible after you return this form.

What could I do to make your work more productive?

What equipment or training do you need to do your best work that you don't have?

What could the company change (add or delete) that would help you do your work better?

What skills and abilities do you have that you think are underutilized?

Any other comments or opinions you would like to express?

Worksheet 7.1 (Continued)
(Part B)

Name _____ Date _____

Job Responsibilities	1–10	Comments

Quality of Work	1–10	Comments
1. Technical skills.		
2. Accuracy, little supervision required.		
3. Creativity/originality of work.		
4. Communication skills.		
5. New approaches to problems.		
6. Accepts responsibility—takes initiative for action.		
7. Forward-thinking/moving in same direction as company.		
8. Continues to learn and improve.		

Quantity of Work	1–10	Comments
1. Meets deadlines.		
2. Consistently hard worker.		
3. Planning/time management/workspace organization.		
4. Does fair share of department's work.		
5. Is in on time, on time to meetings, and doesn't miss a lot of work.		

People Issues/Teamwork	1–10	Comments
1. Solves people problems directly.		
2. Positive influence on coworker morale.		
3. Working relationships inside company.		
4. Leadership in company/shares information and suggestions with others.		
5. Working relationships outside company with customers or vendors.		
6. Participates in meetings.		

Worksheet 7.1 (Continued)

Company Objectives	Department Objectives	Individual Objectives for Next Year

Outstanding Accomplishments/Qualities

Areas for Improvement/Development

to your view of this employee. You can also use this time to do something about the problems the employee hopes will be addressed.

For the second part of the review, fill in the employee's top five job responsibilities, then rate each category from 1 to 10, adding comments where you have something to say. List the employee's "star" moments on the bottom of the second page, along with areas where further training or improvements are needed or desired.

Use the middle of the second page of Worksheet 7.1 to write objectives for the coming year, based on company objectives, and the department objectives you have identified. After the review meeting, give the employee a copy of the worksheet. It's important that you both agree on these objectives and that you meet at least quarterly to discuss them, along with any other areas you identified where improvement is required.

Reality Check

Consider these questions about your completed worksheet:

- Is the company generally supportive of employees who are honestly trying to do their best work?

- Are there a number of employees giving you similar feedback about the company?

- Do the comments reflect a positive feeling about the company, even if many problems are listed, or are there still things that seem to be left unsaid?

- Would you agree with the employee's assessments? Are there things you can do immediately to show you are committed to the employee's success?

- Is your reaction defensive? Do you discount the employee's opinion before you have investigated the concerns? If yes, why?

- Can you objectively review your employees? Do you have favorites for reasons other than their work performance?

- Do your employees have a sense of your vision for them and their work?

- Do you have the courage and organizational support to be honest with your employees about their work performance?

- Do you spend at least 90 minutes preparing for an employee review meeting and at least 90 minutes meeting with the employee?

- Are review sessions a productive meeting of the minds or (1) are they angry and defensive or (2) do they gloss over the real problems?

TEAM FEEDBACK

Worksheet 7.2 is another part of the total 360-degree review process, which is intended to give the employee a full circle of feedback from everyone he or she connects with on the job. There's one caveat to this process—namely, there must be adequate preparation for a company to launch into this process. People who have never received completely honest reviews from their supervisors and who have not had an opportunity to personally evaluate their own strengths and weaknesses are not ready to hear brutally honest comments from their peers and others.

Training with case studies and role playing should be required to give employees both a sense of how to give helpful, constructive, and practical feedback as well as how to accept it when given to you.

The review forms that will be used to solicit feedback should be given to employees three to six months before the process is used. This isn't a surprise inspection—if employees know what standards will be used to measure them, they will begin to change their behavior immediately so that they will not receive negative reviews. If handled this way, you will begin to get the desired result before you even ask for feedback from peers. After all, wouldn't the best result be uniformly positive feedback from happy coworkers?

Making It Happen

The supervisor should give Worksheet 7.2 to a representative number of people who are in a position to review an employee's work. If the coworker reports to the same manager, he or she is considered a team member. If the coworker reports to a different manager, the coworker would be considered a peer. I suggest doing this process twice the first year to give an employee the opportunity to raise his or her score quickly. The scores are usually lowest the first time employees give this feedback review.

When all worksheets are returned, the supervisor should tally an average question score by adding the total of the 1 to 10 scores for each question and dividing that number by the number of people who answered the question. Comments should be collected on another sheet for each question.

Worksheet 7.2
Team Feedback

Please circle your relationship to ——————————————————— (Name)

Team member   Peer

Return this form to ——————— (Date).   (Supervisor) by

Please rate his or her performance in the following categories (10=best).
Your scores and comments will be kept confidential.

Quality of Work	1–10	Comments
1. Technical skills.		
2. Accuracy, little supervision required.		
3. Creativity/originality of work.		
4. Communication skills.		
5. New approaches to problems.		
6. Accepts responsibility—takes initiative for action.		
7. Forward-thinking/moving in same direction as company.		
8. Continues to learn and improve.		

Quantity of Work	1–10	Comments
1. Meets deadlines.		
2. Consistently hard worker.		
3. Planning/time management/workspace organization.		
4. Does fair share of department's work.		
5. Is in on time, on time to meetings, and doesn't miss a lot of work.		

People Issues/Teamwork	1–10	Comments
1. Solves people problems directly.		
2. Positive influence on coworker morale.		
3. Working relationships inside company.		
4. Leadership in company/shares information and suggestions with others.		
5. Working relationships outside company with customers or vendors.		
6. Participates in meetings.		

Comments

The supervisor should meet with the employee to discuss the team feedback results. All feedback should be given confidentially. A total average score of 7 or above for all questions should be considered excellent.

The goal of the meeting should be to look for five items that the employee would like to impact before the next review and to create a strategy for training, development, or more individual feedback (i.e., individual testing or coaching) for that employee.

Reality Check

Consider these questions about your completed worksheet:

- Have you defined the numerical rankings well enough for peers and team members to give meaningful and consistent feedback?

- Do you agree with the feedback given by team members and peers for the employee? Can you help coach the employee to better his or her performance?

- Are you willing to commit the time it will take to make a 360-degree feedback process successful in your company?

- Have you trained employees to know how to give and receive feedback?

- Do you know what characteristics you are looking for in top-level employees? Does this process help you measure for them?

- Are you willing to participate in a 360-degree feedback process yourself? Are you committed to your own development?

MANAGEMENT SKILLS FEEDBACK

Worksheet 7.3 is intended to give feedback to managers on their performance, specifically their people management skills. Although managers are required to give feedback to employees, they may be reticent to get it. Whereas employee performance problems can hurt a company, key manager problems can kill it. It is imperative that managers know that employees will have the opportunity to communicate with senior executives or even the board of directors confidentially.

A company should not attempt to start a 360-degree review process unless all levels of employees are willing to participate equally. Again, managers should know at least three to six months in advance that their subordinates will review their performance. This kind of process can bring to light issues—such as possible sexual harassment or favoritism—early on.

Making It Happen

Ask all subordinates to complete these forms and return them to a senior manager. They should be tallied with an average score per question by adding up the total of the 1 to 10 scores and dividing that number by the number of people who answered the question. Comments should be collected on another sheet by question number.

A senior executive should meet with the manager to discuss the feedback results. It's essential that all feedback be given confidentially without references that would allow the manager to guess the identity of the giver of a particular type of feedback. The intent is the personal and professional growth of the manager, not an opportunity to punish subordinates for their honesty.

An average total score of 7 or above should be considered excellent. The goal of the meeting should be to select five items the manager would like to positively impact before the next review. The company should be willing to provide the resources necessary to make this a priority (individual personality testing, outside coaching) and to create a plan for development.

Worksheet 7.3
Management Skills Feedback

Please rate your supervisor's/manager's performance in the following categories (1–10, 10=best). Your scores and comments will be kept confidential.

Return this form to _____ by _____

	1–10	Comments
Communication		
Makes himself or herself available for communication.		
Is able to communicate honestly.		
Has given me wise suggestions about work or people.		
Is able to gracefully handle my communications.		
Treats everyone fairly (doesn't have pets or favorites).		
Planning		
Manages time wisely.		
Keeps stress level under control.		
Can plan group workload effectively.		
Performance		
Sets appropriate goals for the group.		
Distributes work fairly in our group.		
Sets accountability standards fairly.		
Holds people accountable consistently and fairly.		
Recommends appropriate compensation.		
Feedback		
Gives constructive feedback.		
Controls anger/is not abusive.		
Recognizes outstanding achievement.		
Gives credit to others.		
Leadership		
I respect this person.		
A good example as a role model for our corporate culture.		
Doesn't gossip or allow other behavior which undermines morale.		
Seems happy to be at this company.		
Carries out company rules and supports company policies.		
Other comments you wish to make about your supervisor/manager or about his or her leadership style?		

Reality Check

Consider these questions about your completed worksheet:

- Are managers trained well enough to give and accept feedback?

- Are managers committed to their own development or do they feel they must be unquestionably "right" to lead effectively?

- Do managers see this process as integral to promotional opportunities?

- Are sufficient resources available to employees who want to get the most out of this process, such as outside coaches, mentors, psychologists, personality and skills testing, and training programs for job skills and people skills?

- Is your company paying lip service to professional development, or is it an integral part of your quality program?

EMPLOYEE RANKING SYSTEM

Worksheet 7.4 is intended for confidential use by each department manager as a human resource management tool. It's a place for each manager to record his or her thinking about individual employee performance. It's important to set aside time for managers to discuss their employee-related problems, even if they don't share individual scores. Managers should provide confidential support and feedback for one another in dealing with these critical but challenging management issues.

Making It Happen

Place each employee's initials at the top row of boxes in Worksheet 7.4. Rank each employee from 1 to 10 on each of the dimensions down the left column. At the bottom of each column, total each 1 to 10 score, and divide by the number of categories for an average score. This is just a thumbnail sketch of each of your employees, but the bottom average should give you an indication of top performers and the weaker links in the chain.

Look at your scoring this way: Scores of 8 to 10 indicate your strongest employees. Make sure you are spending enough time mentoring these employees who have the potential to become your next leaders. Most employees will probably fall in the 5 to 7 category and will need a variety of developmental plans. Employees with overall scores of 4 or under have come to a critical point. Can they move up within the next two to three months to a score of 5 or better? If not, you should make the decision to let them go or move them into jobs for which they are better suited. Once you have made this decision, you should let these employees know as soon as possible and do what you can to ease the transition.

Reality Check

Consider these questions about your completed worksheet:

- Are most of your employees in the 6 to 10 range? Are you prepared to take action on employees with lower scores?

- Do you find more performance problems in one category than in others? Are there people problems that could be solved by training?

Worksheet 7.4
Employee Ranking System (by Department)

(1–10, 10=best)

	Employee Number								
	1	2	3	4	5	6	7	8	9
Quality of Work									
1. Technical skills.									
2. Accuracy, little supervision required.									
3. Creativity/originality of work.									
4. Communication skills.									
5. New approaches to problems.									
6. Accepts responsibility—takes initiative for action.									
7. Forward-thinking/moving in same direction as company.									
8. Continues to learn and improve.									
Quantity of Work									
1. Meets deadlines.									
2. Consistently hard worker.									
3. Planning/time management/workspace organization.									
4. Does fair share of department's work.									
5. Is in on time, on time to meetings, and doesn't miss a lot of work.									
People Issues/Teamwork									
1. Solves people problems directly.									
2. Positive influence on coworker morale.									
3. Working relationships inside company.									
4. Leadership in company/shares information and suggestions with others.									
5. Working relationships outside company with customers or vendors.									
6. Participates in meetings.									
Total (A)									
Number of Categories (B)									
Overall Rank (A/B)									

Are they quality or quantity problems that might be due to work overload or inadequate resources?

- Are lower scores due to lack of skills, lack of interest, or lack of willingness to perform up to capacity?

- Are you looking for promotional or other leadership opportunities for employees scoring in the 8 to 10 range?

- Are a few much lower scores bringing down the average for particular employees? Can you give these individuals honest feedback to help them improve these scores?

HUMAN RESOURCE KEY INDICATORS

Worksheet 7.5 allows you to gauge the morale, productivity, and efficiency of the workforce. Generally, absenteeism goes up when employees take vacations in the summer. Watch for higher absenteeism in departments as a possible trend of discontentment.

If you have staffed correctly, temporary labor and overtime should be zero most months or reflect your seasonality. An increase two months in a row could indicate a more regular need that should be filled. Because overtime pay is higher than regular pay, some employees will regularly find reasons to work extra hours. All overtime requests should be approved in advance to keep this extra premium to a minimum.

Tracking trends and asking the right questions should let employees know that you are watching this expense carefully. I also recommend tracking the number of suggestions in the suggestion box as a general indicator of morale problems. If you see a sudden increase, consider it a legitimate concern and take steps, such as an employee survey, to determine the reasons.

Making It Happen

List for each department the number of days missed due to the variety of reasons listed, and get the average days missed per employee by dividing the total days missed by the number of employees. Also determine the amount of money spent on overtime and temporary help by entering the number of hours worked and multiplying by the rate per hour. If you use a suggestion box, tally the number of suggestions and attach them to this worksheet.

Reality Check

Consider these questions about your completed worksheet:

- Are employees in certain departments taking more time off than those in others? Does this suggest anything about the type of work or management that goes on in different departments?

- Are some departments making up for lost time with overtime or temporary help?

Worksheet 7.5
Human Resource Key Indicators
for _____ (Month/Year)

Absenteeism (# of days missed this month)

Department	Vacation	Sick Leave	Personal Leave	Total	Number of Employees	Average/ Employee

Overtime

Department	Number of Overtime Hours	Overtime Premium	Total ($)
		Total:	

Temporary Labor

Department	Number of Hours	Rate ($)/Hours	Total ($)
		Total:	

Attached: Suggestions from Suggestion Box
Total number of suggestions this month _____

- Can efficiency be increased to reduce the need for overtime or temporary labor?

- Are there specific, meaningful connections between fluctuations in human resources indicators and spikes in inventory or order backlogs? If so, what can you do to smooth out these spikes?

WHAT'S NEXT

In the final chapter, I discuss action-based ways for communicating your vision as a leader, as well as tactics for growing your leadership abilities, including the intangibles of what makes for a great CEO.

8

LEADING YOUR BUSINESS FOR MAXIMUM RESULTS

We aim above the mark to hit the mark.
—Ralph Waldo Emerson

When you build a company, you create something that didn't exist before, and it takes a special kind of person to cope with all of the challenges creating a business will bring. It takes both foresight and insight and the ability to look at the world at large and decide where your company must fit in to survive. It also takes insight, the ability to look inside yourself and others, and the willingness to grow personally to meet the ever-increasing demands of running a business. Finally, it takes courage to consistently stay the course when those around you might question your decisions or your actions, as well as the ability to know when you need outside help.

There are 10 factors that help determine whether a business will succeed or fail. In the box on page 232, these factors are not in order of importance; all are essential.

It's no accident that the first five reasons that businesses succeed depend almost exclusively on the CEO and top managers. It's up to you to constantly increase the skills and experience that make you an effective CEO, but the real challenge is to continue growing in the more intangible areas that give you the ability to persist when others would not and the energy to try something new when the last three tries didn't work. The key for this is *maturity*.

TOP 10 REASONS THAT BUSINESSES SUCCEED

1. The experience and skills of the top managers.

2. The energy, persistence, and resourcefulness (the will to make the business succeed) of the top managers.

3. The maturity to treat employees, suppliers, and partners fairly and respectfully.

4. Deal-making skills to sell the product at the highest possible price given your market.

5. Deal-making skills to work with resource suppliers to keep costs low.

6. A product that is at least a cut above the competition, and service that doesn't get in the way of people buying the product.

7. The ability to create a "buzz" around the product with aggressive and strategic marketing.

8. The ability to keep developing new products to retain and build a customer base.

9. Superior location and/or promotion, creating a connection between your product and where it can be obtained.

10. A steady source of business during both good economic times and downturns.

PERSONAL CHARACTERISTICS OF CEOs

There are a number of characteristics that define good CEOs, whether in $5 million or $5 billion companies:

Maturity is a quality that enables you to be willing to risk profits to do the right thing, to have more tolerance for the differences of others, and to be willing to wait until the time is right rather than require immediate gratification.

FIVE DEFINING CHARACTERISTICS OF GREAT CEOS

1. *Personal insight.* Great CEOs are great leaders. They know themselves and what they stand for. They have been called on all their lives as problem solvers because others know them to be fair and impartial. People respect their opinions and look to them for guidance.

    Great CEOs are mature as people. They can suffer disappointment more gracefully than others and give others credit for their achievements. They don't come in the office door yelling for something they need. They aren't as concerned about titles or power structures as they are about the welfare of those who work at the company. They are trustworthy because they've always been honest with people and have earned that trust. They care about families, and they know that people are more important than dollars and express it in their actions every day.

    Finally, great CEOs seek out feedback. They want to know how others see them so that they can understand themselves better and continue to grow as people. They also want feedback about the company from an employee perspective, and they use surveys as a starting point for creating a dialogue to make things better.

2. *Resourcefulness.* Great CEOs seem to have boundless energy. They come to work with the greatest enthusiasm. Even when they don't feel like it, they find ways to reenergize themselves and come in ready to go. They take good care of themselves physically and emotionally so that they can be there for the employees and the needs of the company. They give much more than they take every day.

    They don't give up. If the wall is too high, they back down and find another way around. They don't blame, but they do look for solutions to problems so that those problems are less likely to happen again.

3. *Courage.* The CEO has one of the world's toughest jobs. No matter how tough it was to start the company, it's even harder to keep it going and growing. A CEO must decide what he or she stands for and do what is right, all the time.

(continued)

It takes courage to fire the salesperson responsible for the company's biggest, most lucrative account when that same salesperson drives a company car drunk and causes an accident. There will be many times when CEOs will want to smooth over something that requires decisive action because of the potential consequences or because they just can't take on one more challenge at the moment. However, CEOs who exercise poor moral judgment will lose their personal integrity with all of their employees watching.

4. *Willing to look at risk.* A great CEO isn't afraid to look at the downside and answer the hard questions he or she hopes will never become a reality. The CEO needs a backup plan—one that is designed by looking at the company's worst-case scenarios. This plan addresses questions such as: What if your industry experiences a slump? What if new governmental regulations affect your business? What if you lose the client that accounts for 50 percent of your sales?

   Preparing yourself and your company for these eventualities may be the difference between a tough year or two and bankruptcy. If you are in business for 20 years, some of your worst-case scenarios will probably happen. The key is to be ready and able to take immediate action to reduce the loss.

5. *Foresight.* It seems some CEOs have an uncanny ability to predict the future. They may have unusual insights into their particular markets, and luck may play a part as well. In addition, they are prepared to create their own luck by cultivating an ability to see opportunities for their company and to make the deals that convert those opportunities into realities. Some things that may seem like amazing foresight are actually the result of the hard work and discipline it takes to constantly look forward to build a successful company.

   Great CEOs must also constantly develop new products to build and retain a customer base. Foresight is also the ability to hire and retain the right people, looking ahead toward the growth of the company. Finally, over time, each company must develop a steady source of business during both good economic times and bad, because there are sure to be bad economic times during the life of a business.

FACING THE TOUGHEST QUESTIONS

One CEO who demonstrates many of the traits I mentioned is Toby Lenk, who took his company, eToys, from a start-up to a public company in just two years. On the day the company went public in May 1999, Lenk's 10.5 million shares of stock were worth more than $850 million. However, when eToys filed for bankruptcy in March 2001, Lenk still held 10 million shares of eToys stock. He ended up with the money he took in salary for those four years and little else—even though his idea made a lot of other people very wealthy.

Lenk's story is a great study about CEOs and raises some provocative questions: How much do you give; how much do you take? What do you owe the company you build, and what does it owe you? Where do you go to find the answers?

Great CEOs like Lenk confront difficult questions like these and follow their moral and ethical compasses. They create both a compelling and heartfelt business plan and game plan. Ultimately, their behavior and their belief in their vision for the company will determine whether the endeavor thrives or perishes.

LOOK TO THE LONG TERM—THE VERY LONG TERM

A crucial aspect of leading your business is to determine how to keep the business running in your absence. You won't be around forever, so plan ahead. This fact is sometimes difficult to appreciate, especially if you founded the company, but it's important. Making sure that your company survives helps you and your employees focus on matters of importance.

Many companies run, and even thrive, on personality alone—on the charismatic leader whose employees rally round for direction and inspiration. However, businesses like these can appear more like cults than companies, and cult companies often don't outlive their leaders. Companies thrive when they operate according to principles their employees can believe in. Your employees will do better if they believe that your company exists to do something more than make you wealthy. They want to know that their efforts will pay off whether you're around or not.

This doesn't take away from you—the person running the company—so much as it gives to your employees. You improve your own prospects for a payoff from your employees if you improve their prospects for a payoff from your company. If you show them that you expect your company to run whether you're there or not, you demonstrate that you really do look to the long term.

FIND THE IMPORTANT DETAILS AND FOCUS ON THEM

Another aspect of leadership is knowing what drives your business. Study your operations; then extract those details that are key to your success. It's not enough to house volumes of reports on a bookshelf. You must know what those reports mean. If, for example, you send out 50,000 pieces of direct mail and two weeks later sales jump, you may conclude that you dropped an effective mailing. However, perhaps your advertising kicked in at the same time, or perhaps a distributor launched an incentive program. You must find out so you know what works and what doesn't.

In addition, remember that data is often about quantity, not quality. Only people—not mere data—can qualitatively measure performance by answering questions such as the following:

- How well do our results match up against our expectations? What's different?

- Is the trend up or down?

- Will these trends last a short time, or do they look long term?

- What might have contributed to what we see in the data?

- What's missing from this data that would lead us to ask more questions?

As a rule, the finance department is the sole corporate unit devoted to quantitative analysis. It doesn't develop, produce, market, or deliver the product. It measures the results of your efforts to do those things. It provides you with data from which to draw the benchmarks for measuring your company's performance. This doesn't make the financial department more important than the others, but simply more useful in this context—if you decide to use it this way.

FACE REALITY WHEN YOU LOOK AT YOUR COMPANY DATA

The problems you encounter in running your company are tough enough to solve. Don't let confusion muddy the waters. This means keeping your analyses as objective as possible and admitting what you see to those around you. Don't try to persuade yourself or others to see what isn't there. You may be the only person, for example, who can tell whether a two-month downturn in revenues reflects your ordinary business cycle or the beginning of a more drastic trend. Therefore, you must gauge the truth and act accordingly. Later in this chapter, I discuss how to know if you can help to fix this trend by bringing in an outside consultant.

LEADING DURING TIMES OF GROWTH

Your business may outperform your projections, or it may fall short. Either way, you need to know. A game plan allows you to monitor performance in detail, so learn how performance varies from the vision of your business plan. There are no shortcuts in preparing the information, in studying it, and in acting on it. You must plan, act, measure, and plan again. Don't expect to do this quickly. Analyzing the data takes time—at least twice as long as it takes to compile the data, according to one rule of thumb.

You may be jubilant when you outperform expectations, but just as many problems can stem from too much business as too little. Are you prepared with staff and resources to handle faster growth than you initially projected?

Take each variance as an opportunity to rethink how it will impact each aspect of your business. Although growth can be a wonderful thing for a company, it can be challenging. This is a great time to get some outside consulting help from someone who has been there and can guide you in the next step for your company.

To be sure you stay on track, you will need to keep data and make choices in each of two areas: where to invest your time and resources over time. Running a small business is a balancing act because resources are always scarce. I always set out to upgrade and change each area over time—

finance, sales and marketing, operations, human resources—so that no area would be left without improvements for a long period.

Managing high growth means you have done many important things well—product development, marketing, and sales—that's the good news. The bad news is that, at least for the short run, it feels as though the company is running you. Sometimes the best you can do is to enjoy the ride. Understand that it's probably temporary and leverage the opportunities as best you can.

What you do during this period will have an impact on the life of your company. Watch for the following:

- Don't reduce your quality standards or treat people as if they are dispensable.

- Avoid burnout (yours and your employees'). Keep this time in perspective and help your employees do the same by taking time off when you can.

- Consider getting a line of credit or other borrowing vehicle while your sales and profits can justify it.

- Consider the risks of stocking more inventory than you can quickly sell in case demand decreases faster than expected.

- Get all the public relations you can while your story is newsworthy.

- Pay down debt and set up the ability to borrow in the future.

MANAGING SLUMPS

If you plan to stay in business long, you'll see up economies and down economies in your career. The secret of success is to learn how to make money during both. This means trying brand new, bold strategies. Determine who's still buying what you're selling; maybe they are in a new industry, or the product they're buying is just a little different from what you're offering.

The good news about lean times is that they might offer you a breather from the otherwise breakneck speed at which you usually operate. For example, you'll have time to plan that marketing campaign you've been thinking about for the past two years.

It's essential to stay positive in tough times and to celebrate the progress you've already made in your business and the lean times you've already made it through. Instead of looking at today and next week, look at a year or more ago. What have you done that you're particularly proud of in the past few years? Resist the impulse to conclude that your success is now ending—a slump is just a lull in the action.

Ask really successful people and you'll find that most have gone to the edge of personal crisis. It's what they learned about themselves during those critical times that made it all worthwhile. Have you been tested in the past? Do you know you will be able to make it because you've risen to the challenge before?

If not, maybe this is the time to find out about yourself. If you usually shrink from a challenge, this time rise to meet it. Find the big customers you've always wanted but assumed you were too small to lure—ask them for their business, or do something really bold to get yourself noticed.

You'll never find the energy for that next bold move unless you feel good about yourself right now. Indeed, you're too important to the business you've created not to take great care of yourself. Learn what works for you and do it religiously. Get physical activity, even if it's just a walk during lunch. Develop eating habits that will sustain you. Find the things you enjoy and engage in them regularly. Get outside perspectives so that you don't take everything so seriously.

YOU CAN'T DO IT ALONE

The job of a CEO is overwhelming—so overwhelming, that many CEOs don't realize that they've lost touch with their families, lost friends, and haven't done anything but work for years.

Don't try to run a company without support. If your family thinks the business is a bad idea altogether, try to get some counseling and talk it through. It's perfectly understandable that a spouse might be concerned that a business will cost money initially, be risky, and, more importantly, take you away from the family. This isn't an insignificant concern. Continually work on compromises.

Well-established companies face family concerns as well. Who should work in the family business? Who in the next generation should run the business after the founder retires? How can the family wealth be divided after the death of the founder if all of the wealth is in the business? Many other CEOs have dealt with these issues successfully, and you can, too, with their help. Find a group of other CEOs, preferably from a variety of industries, to share the burden with you and to give you the benefit of their experiences and help you cultivate new ideas.

GETTING OUTSIDE HELP

In addition to finding other CEOs for guidance, you might find yourself needing the services of a consultant at certain points during the life of your business. Many owners and managers are suspicious of consultants; they distrust freelance experts who charge big hourly rates but make little long-term commitment. Sometimes, they resent any outsider criticizing their companies—no matter how much they know, intellectually, that they need help. However, one crucial trait of great leaders is that they know when to ask for help.

REASONS YOU MIGHT NEED SOME OUTSIDE HELP

- You need a high or specific level of expertise that goes beyond what your company could afford to pay an employee.

- Your needs, generated by growth or external market forces, are only temporary.

- Problems have become so acute that they require immediate response.

- Problems are of such a broad institutional nature that they defy internal response.

How do you know you're in this kind of position? You're calling the bank every day—nervous to hear your account balance because you can't get straight information from your accounting department. Traditional marketing campaigns that have worked for years take a sudden dive in performance. Production bottlenecks you never saw before flare up and won't go away.

Unfortunately, identifying a problem isn't the same as fixing it. That's where outside consultants—used well—come in. To use a consultant well, you have to look past short-term tensions to long-term goals. You have to be willing to share relevant information freely and cooperate openly. This doesn't mean handing over the keys to your kingdom, but it does mean you have to do some preliminary work and expand your concepts of trust and comfort to include some outsiders.

Done well, these efforts will return many times their original investment. They'll get you past sticky problems and lead you into productive relationships with the best consultants in their fields. Consultants have a bad reputation among some owners and managers for two basic reasons:

1. There are many bad ones.

2. Many clients use consultants badly.

HIRING QUALITY CONSULTING HELP

In the 1980s, the number of business consultants, especially financial consultants, grew substantially. There are many business experts happy to work with small, growing companies. However, as a potential buyer, you should beware. Not every consultant is a McKinsey Co. or Tom Peters.

Erratic use makes problems of erratic quality worse. Often, the owners and managers who complain most about consultants use them in the most ill-advised ways. Horror stories usually include some variation on this theme: A manager knows someone or meets someone whose ideas and expertise impress people (primarily, the manager himself or herself). The someone may be a consultant or may become available because of a career change. The manager likes the someone's ideas or energy or charisma but doesn't have a suitable job available, so the manager hires the someone as a consultant on some nonspecific basis such as "improving performance." A scenario like this is destined for trouble.

If you want people with good ideas and energy and charisma around you, hire them as employees. Save consultants for more specific goals.

Finding the Right Consultant

Most consultants market their services by word of mouth. As a result, when owners or managers think they need someone, they usually do best to ask friends or peers for names, but recommendations don't ensure success. The key to success lies in interviewing consultants well and being very specific about your needs, expectations, and budget.

The following questions and answer guidelines can help you interview prospective consultants and choose the right one for a given time and circumstance.

Ten Questions You Should Ask before Hiring a Consultant

1. *Most consultants focus on two areas: cutting costs and raising revenues. What do you see as the relationship between the two functions? Which do you do better?*

Cost cutting is the consultant's usual expertise. It's what most companies need. The main reason for corporate restructuring is to reduce costs. Many hire outside consultants to take an objective look at organizational charts, value-adding processes, and competitive environments. "We spend a lot of time talking to a company's customers, so we understand what they like and don't like," one consultant says. "What does the customer value? Is it time? Is it quality? We define that." This means that a company can cut jobs and still not touch on one nonvalue-added activity or add value to the customer.

2. *What was your professional experience before you became a consultant?*

Ultimately, you should want any consultant you use to have a strong bottom-line sensibility. You want this person—or team—to focus on the things that will add the greatest amount of value to your company in the shortest amount of time. This kind of thinking doesn't come naturally to many people. It usually demands two kinds of experience: as a chief executive officer or as a corporate-turnaround specialist. A consultant who has this kind of experience has dealt with strict cost controls, high-pressure scrutiny, and the need for quick results. These are the same traits you should look for in anyone giving you expert advice. Though it may seem counterintuitive, you might look for bankruptcy and similar workout experience from a consultant. The urgency learned in that environment applies well to the urgencies of daily business life.

3. *How many professionals work with you or at your firm?*

Business consultants fall essentially into two categories: solo practitioners and team players. The differences between the two usually involve the type of work they take. Most of the time, the soloists deal with less specific, strategic, or vision-related issues; the teams get into more tightly focused number crunching. Less specific functions tend to take less time (sometimes as little as one day); the more specific take more.

One of these functions isn't better or worse than the other. The trap to beware is the marketing soloist who claims he or she can also review all of your accounting. The exercises in this book will help you make your financial statements easier to understand, but don't expect one consultant to fix all your problems.

4. *Will you sign a letter of confidentiality? Will you refrain from working for our competitors?*

Some owners and managers assume that short-term strategic consultants pose less of a threat to proprietary interests than the number crunchers. However, you and your staff should feel free to discuss any business subject with your consultant and trust his or her discretion. If you feel uncomfortable, you won't discuss things candidly. The solution is to ask all consultants to sign a letter of confidentiality.

Your risk in these cases isn't usually that the consultant will knowingly steal proprietary information or material. Most are professional enough and work in small enough markets that reputations matter. More often, the risk involves a consultant's unwittingly mentioning something. If the consultant has signed a confidentiality letter, he or she will be more likely to think twice.

5. *Who are some of your other clients? Who are some people and companies with whom you've worked before? May I call them to ask about your work?*

Don't be wowed by big-shot former clients. At big companies, consultants are hired in teams to tackle extremely specific projects. Just because the person in the expensive suit claims Chrysler as a former client doesn't mean he knows Lee Iacocca on a first-name basis. In fact, it's better if the consultant has worked with companies closer to your size and shape because he or she will more likely understand your needs.

6. *With how many clients do you work at one time? Do you have enough time to devote to our company to accomplish our goals? Will you return phone calls or e-mails the same day?*

Asking other or former clients about the consultant's responsiveness and attentiveness can be helpful, as can asking more pointed questions of the consultant. The questions all focus on the same point: How much attention can the consultant afford to spend on your needs? The number of clients a consultant can serve well varies with the kind of service provided and client involved, but some general rules apply: You want to have same-day response to questions or problems. If you're undertaking a major restructuring, you probably don't want your consultant working with more than two or three other clients. One caveat is that some owners and managers who've had experiences with overly invasive (and expensive) consultants warn that you shouldn't be the only client a consultant has.

7. *Will you teach us to do this work for ourselves and become self-sufficient? How long will this take?*

One common trap in using a consultant is becoming dependent on him or her. From the consultant's perspective, this may simply be good business, ensuring future work. From your perspective, it may be little better than the status you had before you had the consultant come in. By making training part of the consultant's job, you can limit the chances of a prolonged engagement. Establish a schedule within which the consultant can accomplish his or her goals. Assign a staff person to work closely in this process and learn everything he or she can.

8. *Have you written anything—published or not—that deals with issues such as the ones this company faces?*

Consultants love to write about their experiences and their theories. If so, it can help you understand how the consultant sees markets and business factors that may affect you. Management or technical literature can be a good place to look for consultants. Although the latest management guru writing for the *Harvard Business Review* may be beyond your needs and means, you might be able to find useful experts in trade or regional newspapers and journals.

9. *How do you charge for services? Do your fees include travel time and other miscellaneous charges or are those billed separately?*

There's no set standard for paying consultants: Some work on a straight-fee basis, others work for a fee plus performance bonus, and a few work on a contingency basis—tied to sales increases or cost reductions. As with paying any outside contractor, your concerns should be ensuring a high quality of work and containing costs within a predetermined budget. With consultants, focusing their use as specifically as possible will help accomplish both of these ends.

In addition, make it clear from the beginning what incidental expenses you're willing to pay and how you'll pay them. Consultants who've worked at or for large corporations may be accustomed to expense accounts that you aren't. Be very clear about how much you're willing to spend on the whole project or series of projects. Insist that the consultant warn you—in writing—if the project won't be completed on time and within budget.

10. *What kind of documentation will you give us when the project is completed? Who will own that documentation?*

Keeping a paper trail of the work a consultant does for you accomplishes several ends—all good. First, if the consultation has worked well, this will usually give you some forms and tools to use to improve some part of your performance.

Second, it allows you to keep a record of the analyses made of your company and the responses you've taken. This kind of "scrapbook" can be a big help when dealing with future problems or other consultants. Finally, keeping a paper trail makes clear what the consultant did—and didn't do—while working for you. If any disputes should emerge over payment, ownership, or confidentiality, you'll have some support.

In general, all of the work (including spreadsheets, working papers, plans, or literature) a consultant does for you is your property. Sometimes—especially in the cases of innovations and literature—this becomes an issue. Make it clear from the beginning that you want to own everything that comes from the consultation.

Establishing a Successful Relationship

Talk to as many consultants as you can before hiring one. Even if you have one person or firm in mind, interview at least a few others as a sort of due diligence. You'll probably find that each interview helps you focus on the issues you're hiring a consultant to help resolve.

Conduct the interviews in a comfortable place. In some cases, this might mean a neutral location and setting—over lunch or in some kind of recreational setting. Being away from the office sometimes helps people think about problems in more objective terms.

When you've found a consultant who seems promising, use the interview to test his or her response to one or two of the real problems you're facing. You don't have to recreate every detail of your problem; boil it down to its essential elements and pose it as a sample of the kind of work you're anticipating.

This kind of question works on two levels. First, it gives you a sense of how the consultant works in a short amount of time with rudimentary information. Second, it lets you know what kind of response the consultant gives. You can judge these things on a personal level as well as a professional level. Ask yourself if this is the kind of person with whom you'd feel comfortable working. Does the consultant respond quickly enough? Does he or she think carefully enough? Is he or she too reserved? Too extreme?

Working intensely with an outside critic and analyst of your company requires a certain level of personal affinity—at least some similarity in style. Although you don't have to (and probably shouldn't) have a personal relationship with a consultant, you shouldn't underestimate the importance of professional compatibility.

A good consultant will relate to your company and your goals and make immediate contributions. Sometimes the best work a consultant does comes when he or she is new to your company.

Interviewing consultants carefully also helps you avoid wasting their time—and your own—later on. Using a consultant effectively and well depends to a significant degree on how you set the relationship up initially. The following steps explain this process more succinctly.

Do Your Homework before the Consultant Comes In

Too many owners and managers hire a consultant and then stop thinking. They present a list of general problems and expect the expert to conjure dramatic results. This approach almost always ends in frustration and many, many billable hours.

Instead, you have to take the initiative. Discuss your needs, problems, and parameters in candid terms from the start. Set a budget or schedule upfront for each project a consultant tackles. Save your skepticism (or your staff's) for the interview process; once you've chosen a consultant, give him or her everything you've got.

Know What You Need from the Consultant

One of the biggest cost drivers in hiring outside expertise is bringing people up to date on your company's operations. It's a cost driver that you can control, though. However, it's important for the consultant to stay away from data gathering and other basic reporting functions; keep the consultant focused on analysis. You can tabulate numbers yourself; you've hired the expert to help you move forward from there. If you're able to keep records over even a short period of time, you can hand the consultant your paper trail and ask him or her to read the performance numbers directly. The worksheets in this book are designed to serve that purpose.

Another point to consider is that many consultants have a steep sort of half life as to enthusiasm for a project. In other words, their best thoughts and greatest creativity come early in their relationships with clients. Being prepared from the start allows you to take full advantage of short attention spans.

When you hire consultants, keep in mind that their most important skill should be critical analysis and problem solving.

Give consultants specific goals. Don't just say you have problems. In short, know what you need, whether it's a temporary executive, an outside thinker to help jump-start your ideas, or an arbitrator for internal disputes.

In addition, to the extent you use consultants as managers, try to limit them to so-called "bridge management" functions. *Bridge management* simply means an outside consultant will oversee a business function between permanent managers or during periods of particular turmoil.

The following are reasons that owners and managers hire bridge managers:

- They need someone to handle excess workloads caused by projects or increased business.

- They need someone to bridge the gaps left when downsizing takes place.

- They want to test the need for a position or the person being considered for hire.

- They want someone to handle specific short-term tasks that call for experience and objectivity.

Make sure to give bridge managers clear instructions and schedules for the work they will do.

Have Deadlines

You should also give them short deadlines or even a series of short deadlines instead of open-ended ones. Consultants may serve operational functions for set periods of time, but they shouldn't manage in the broad sense of that word.

Like any outside contractor or vendor, consultant services are a commodity—and consultants want to sell as much of this commodity over as long a time as they can. That's their understandable inclination as business people. However, it's your understandable inclination as an owner or manager to minimize the amount you pay them.

The consultant may be right to say there aren't quick fixes to serious problems, but don't let that lead to open-ended engagements. Most consultants agree that restructuring involves two phases: a design phase, in which new ways of doing work are fashioned, and an implementation phase, in which the new ways of doing work actually are put in place. Have the consultant schedule these phases. This helps set up an exit strategy for the consultant, which is an important cost control tool. In addition, the consultant will see the project as a limited engagement, rather than open ended.

Keep the Hierarchy Clear

Have the consultant report to the fewest people possible—one, if that can be arranged. As we've discussed elsewhere, the best way to do this is to keep the agenda simple and clear. When you hire a consultant, write a short memo that tells the relevant people in your company who this person is and why you've hired him or her. Also specify where and how the consultant fits into the organizational chart. Avoid confusion of authority and responsibility.

A consultant who worked as a bridge manager for a North Carolina bank in the early 1990s found that two factors ensured success. First, the senior manager made sure that everyone affected was informed of her arrival and her background, which gave her instant credibility. Second, the terms of her appointment were clearly spelled out. "I had a contract, and I treated the job as if it were my own, but I clearly knew that this was only for a certain period," she says.

Keep the Consultant Focused on Value-Added Functions

Make sure the consultant has both a vision for how to improve your company and a clear sense of concrete ways to help your company. The consultant's image of operational perfection may sound great in a management journal, but it may do little in the marketplace. For example, consultants often focus on staffing and personnel issues as a means of increasing efficiency. However, that's not always the best approach to take. If your product costs $10 to produce with labor costs of $1 and you cut out half the labor cost (a major achievement), you've still reduced your cost by only 5 percent. If the retail price of your product is $20, you've cut only 2.5 percent. The consultant will boast that he or she has cut labor costs in half—but the retail customer won't be so impressed by this discount. Ultimately, processes that don't add value to the customer erode a company's competitiveness.

Set Regular Meetings

Set regular times to meet (weekly or monthly) when the consultant will review conclusions, answer questions, and challenge you on better ways to run your business.

Make sure these are working meetings. Avoid meetings that turn into administrative updates. By meeting with the consultant regularly, you can compartmentalize—and better control—the amount of time you spend with him or her. It also forces the consultant to be succinct and not draw on too much of your time. In this context, you can expect more from a consultant than from an employee. The consultant's attention should focus squarely on problems you're paying him or her to consider, not on operational details.

This approach may not be practical in the midst of an intense project, but it will be a good way to use the consultant before and after that intensity. (Also bear in mind that not all consulting relationships have to be intense at any point in their duration.)

Don't Tolerate Vague Conclusions

Because consulting is a business that relies on a constant stream of new ideas, some consultants become immersed in trendy terms. For example, phrases such as "business process innovation," "business process re-assessment," "core process redesign," and "business process reengineering" all mean the same thing: restructuring your company. Some financial and management consultants revel in technical language and jargon. It's an easy way of making themselves appear better informed and qualified than one another—and potential clients. This can present a bewildering array of information and advice. Wise people, from Benjamin Franklin to Stephen Hawking, have said that true intelligence is the ability to explain complicated concepts in simple terms.

Remember that consultants you hire work for you. They should answer the questions you ask in language you prefer. Insist that they do.

Specific Applications for Consultants

Here are some more detailed uses owners and managers often find for consultants:

- Running focus groups drawn from your customers.

- Producing or reviewing long-term strategic plans.

- Analyzing divestitures, mergers, or acquisitions.

- Changing the methods by which performance is rewarded.

- Helping you use technology more effectively.

- Interviewing your employees to help you discover how they feel about the direction of the company.

- Assessing the effectiveness of your staff and analyzing your workforce.

- Proposing new staffing mixes, which bring together individuals who contribute to a particular solution.

- Changing job descriptions to lower costs, reduce waste, and improve the quality of products and services.

- Speaking to your board of directors or lenders to increase management's credibility.

- Finding investors or other sources of equity funding.

In conclusion, when you keep consultants disciplined and focused, you can use them to great advantage.

BOARDS OF DIRECTORS AND ADVISORS

Very few business people have all the expertise they need to successfully run a business alone. In addition to using consultants, most successful business owners have had mentors, support groups, or boards of advisors to offer advice and support on critical issues at times of both challenge and opportunity. These business leaders recognize that it would be foolish to deprive themselves of all the help they can get.

If you're incorporated, you are required to have a board of directors. The directors may be friends or family, and you generally aren't required to have more than two or three directors if you run a small,

---

TEN QUESTIONS TO ASK YOUR BOARD OF DIRECTORS

1. What do you want the company to accomplish in the years ahead?

2. Do you think the company is currently missing any opportunities it ought to be pursuing?

3. What messages would you like to send to the staff in terms of your own philosophies about your business?

4. What would you like a planning process to accomplish for you and for the company?

5. In your estimation, what are the key internal problems facing the company right now?

6. What could really hurt the business in the next few years?

7. Do you want to incorporate any plans to change ownership into the planning process?

8. How much involvement would you like to have/plan to have in the company this year?

9. What insights do you have about the future of our industry?

10. Are there other comments or opinions you would like to have integrated into the planning process?

privately-owned company. You can use a board of directors to help with a variety of decisions and strategic moves. To start the dialog, make sure to get the answers to these questions each year, particularly before you start a strategic or annual planning process.

You can also seek out other talent by using professional advisors (i.e., your attorney, accountant, insurance agent) and by setting up a board of advisors.

A board of advisors is usually composed of four to eight individuals, each of whom brings a different type of expertise (marketing, finance, operations, product or service expertise, human resource, strategy, etc., in your industry or not).

Consider potential board sources from these categories:

- Trade associations.

- Government or educational institutions.

- Successful entrepreneurs.

- Suppliers.

- Professionals in your industry.

- Other professionals (attorneys, accountants, insurance agents, real estate brokers, bankers, consultants).

A board of advisors is not the same as a board of directors. A board of directors has a legal responsibility to the shareholders of a corporation.

A board of advisors has no legal obligation to make decisions—it is created solely to give advice to the business owner. Advisors, therefore, don't have the same personal liability as directors.

It's especially important for a new business to set up a board of advisors. It can help with funding, both in raising funds and in giving the kind of credibility to the enterprise that lenders and investors like to see.

Boards of advisors usually meet quarterly. Help your board help you by setting an agenda for the meeting and sending the board information on how the company is doing ahead of time. Plan to meet for about three hours per session. Your agenda should include all the major questions you would like to have help in answering, both problems you are wrestling with and upcoming opportunities.

In addition to the quarterly meetings, advisors should expect to be available to you by phone and should also be expected to review monthly reports or updates and telephone you with their questions. Advisors will probably spend about 10 hours per quarter on your business.

If you are a start-up business, advisors may agree to meet without pay. Once you have completed your first year in business or if you had outside funding from the start, plan to pay advisors anywhere from $1,000 to $2,500 per quarter, usually right after the quarterly meeting.

STARTING OVER: THE ANNUAL GAME-PLANNING PROCESS

No matter how often you do strategic planning, you need a new game plan every year. The first step is to accumulate and review the right kinds of background information about what's already been accomplished—in particular, data that show trends up or down over time—such as meaningful sales, operational, and financial reports—and feedback from outside the entrepreneur's limited vision. You can generally gather feedback in the form of surveys: from customers, vendors, business partners, and employees. Having this knowledge as mental background is important to planning for the future. All participants should have this information for review two weeks before a planning day or multiple day retreat. It is best if each participant holds the responsibility for preparing some of the material in the notebook.

Action planning must come from a consensus on the major challenges and opportunities facing the business. Issues should be labeled as critical (needing immediate task force action), to be dealt with this year, and left for attention later when resources are available. Critical issues might be cash flow and negative perceptions of product or service. All agreed-on objectives must be doable with the resources and time allotted, or the plan is destined for failure.

TOOLS FOR LEADING YOUR BUSINESS

The worksheets at the end of this chapter can help you get feedback that will be invaluable in making you a better leader. These resources will help you to see trends from year to year. You can also use these tools for developing your plan for improving morale and making yourself a resource in helping employees get their jobs done. These resources include:

- Employee opinion survey.
- Company performance review.

Ask yourself these questions about your role in the company and its success:

- Where are you spending your time, now or during the next two months?
- How do you enhance your own personal creativity?
- Does the business play to your strengths?
- What are your top five accomplishments (in business or not)?
- What are your top three weaknesses as a business owner?
- Do you work more than six days a week or 50 hours a week?
- What are your hobbies?
- How much time per week do you spend with family and friends?
- Who holds you accountable for your work as a CEO?
- If you could change one thing in your business, what would it be?
- What is the one thing really bothering you most in your business right now?

EMPLOYEE OPINION SURVEY

Worksheet 8.1 is a traditional opinion survey, meant to be used at about the same time each year and trended over time. Add questions as they seem pertinent to particular areas of concern.

Making It Happen

Ask employees to complete this form and return it via e-mail or on paper. It can be done anonymously. Tally a score for each question by adding up the total 1 to 10 scores and dividing by the number of responses with that question answered. Congratulate yourselves on scores of 8 to 10. Plan to work throughout the year to increase scores of 5 to 7. Items scored 4 or under must be considered high priority items, and you should consider assembling task forces to find solutions immediately. This holds true except for compensation issues where scores of 4 and 5 are to be expected; 3 or under should be investigated.

Always give employees feedback about overall scores as soon as possible—at least within two weeks. Keep comments grouped by type on a separate sheet. Respond to those who ask for a personal response by letter or meeting within two weeks, as well.

Reality Check

Consider these questions about your completed worksheet:

- After ranking your problem areas by type in the survey, are they what you expected?

- Are there steps you can take to immediately show your concern for employees and their concerns?

- Are long-term problems, such as an unworkable facility or inadequate benefits, being dealt with? Are employees aware of the progress?

- Are employees generally upbeat about the company?

- Has employee morale improved or worsened over time?

Worksheet 8.1
Employee Opinion Survey

Directions: Please read the following statements, and check the response that is closest to your opinion or attitude (10 = strongly agree, 5 = have no opinion, 1 = strongly disagree).

Return to _____ by _____.

Physical Facilities

___ 1. For my area, the lighting, ventilation, and general working conditions are very good.

___ 2. Other than my own computer, the supplies and machines I use are very good.

___ 3. The computer hardware and software I use fill my needs very well.

___ 4. Safety conditions here are very good.

___ 5. My work space (desk, etc.) provides me with a lot of room to work.

Compensation/Benefits

___ 6. For what I do, the pay is fair.

___ 7. The reasons for getting or not getting a raise are very clear.

___ 8. My pay here is higher than that for the same work at other organizations.

___ 9. The insurance benefits are as good as other organizations'.

___ 10. I have a clear understanding of all the benefits the company provides.

My Job/Supervisor

___ 11. My on-the-job training has been very good.

___ 12. The instructions that my supervisor gives me are always clear.

___ 13. The amount of freedom I have to do a good job is all I need.

___ 14. My last performance review with my supervisor was very helpful and informative.

___ 15. I think I am supervised not too closely, but just about right.

___ 16. The amount of feedback our department gets as to how we're doing is very good.

___ 17. I always know what my supervisor expects from me.

___ 18. I always feel secure in telling my supervisor what I think.

___ 19. My supervisor has pets and favorites.

___ 20. When handling discipline, my supervisor is always fair.

___ 21. My supervisor handles my complaints and problems very well.

___ 22. I am never unfairly criticized by my supervisor.

___ 23. The amount of work expected of me is considerable, but within reason.

___ 24. My supervisor always gives me credit for a good job when I do one.

___ 25. Overall, my supervisor always does his/her job.

Company Climate/Teamwork/Future

___ 26. I find my work satisfying.

___ 27. If I do good work, my job is secure.

___ 28. The people I work with get along well together.

___ 29. There is not enough cooperation between my department and other departments.

___ 30. I have pride in our organization.

Worksheet 8.1 (Continued)

_____ 31. If a good friend should ask me about a job here, I would strongly urge him/her to work here.

_____ 32. For those who want to, there are opportunities to get ahead.

_____ 33. I think my future here is very bright and secure.

_____ 34. Employees are fairly selected for promotion.

_____ 35. I can trust top management to be fair.

_____ 36. The opportunities to talk to management, other than my supervisor, are many.

_____ 37. Top management seems to enforce company rules and policies appropriately.

_____ 38. I think top management is sincerely interested in the employees.

Considering all the questions, the one area where I most want to see improvement is (write in the number of the question).

Comments on areas that weren't covered by this survey:

Other comments.

☐ I'd like a personal response to my survey.   Name _____

☐ I'd rather remain anonymous.

COMPANY PERFORMANCE REVIEW

The Employee Opinion Survey (Worksheet 8.1) seeks to understand employee comfort and morale. The Company Performance Review (Worksheet 8.2) asks employees to rate behaviors that could kill a company over time if left unchecked. The purpose of Worksheet 8.2 is to determine the ethical issues of concern in the corporate culture. It should not be given the same time the Employee Opinion Survey is distributed.

All of the items in the questions have done tremendous damage to companies in the past. They all pertain to the actions of individuals, which may be unknown, known, or even condoned by the organization. The CEO's setting standards for acceptable work behavior and the managers' walking this talk are the only means for solving problems in these areas.

This review must be completed anonymously, or employees won't be comfortable answering honestly. The object is to make all employees suddenly more aware that actions that are sometimes common in companies can do real and lasting damage. It takes effort to increase the recognition of ethical issues to make it easier to begin setting standards.

Making It Happen

The directions on Worksheet 8.2 ask employees to fill in one column at a time with either a 1 or 2. The first column asks whether a particular behavior should be considered (in the employee's opinion) ethical or unethical, right or wrong. The second column asks employees whether this behavior is exhibited at the company.

The most serious problems (again, in the opinion of the employee) will be those with a score of 1 in the first column and also 1 in the second. The company doesn't need to be concerned with any questions in which scores of 2 in the first column and 2 in the second column are uniformly present.

Reality Check

Consider these questions about your completed worksheet:

- Are there ethical issues you uncovered with this survey that surprised and concerned you?

Worksheet 8.2
Company Performance Review

Please help us improve the performance of our company by taking the time to give some feedback. The first time you go through this review, please only pay attention to column 1 and write in the number 1 or the number 2, depending on how you think the behavior described should be perceived (not whether you find it here at the company) (1 = this is wrong, 2 = this really isn't a problem).

After you have numbers filled in in column 1, fill in column 2 by indicating how we behave here at our company in relation to the behavior described (1 = yes, 2 = no).

	Column 1	Column 2
Employees …		
Don't give a full days work for a full days pay.		
Take office supplies home.		
Use the organization's telephone, fax, computer, photocopier for personal use.		
Accept gifts or favors from suppliers.		
Distort or falsify internal reports.		
Fill out time sheets with less than 100% accuracy.		
Gossip about other employees.		
Pad expense reports.		
Plan company-paid trips around personal needs to travel.		
Use company vehicles for personal errands.		
Use company letterhead for personal correspondence.		
Backdate reports or other documents to make it appear they complied with procedures or completed work on time.		
Say nothing when others are obviously violating rules.		
Undermine morale.		
Hold outside jobs that may have a conflicting interest.		
Do other work on this company's time or with its equipment.		
Supervisors/Managers …		
Discriminate by gender or race in hiring, promotion, or pay.		
Abuse employees.		
Deal inappropriately with ill or injured employees.		
Allow or rationalize unsafe or unhealthy working conditions.		
Discourage internal criticism about unfair activities.		
Fail to give timely an honest performance reviews.		
Fail to give promised salary increases.		
Inadequately train employees.		
Do not allow appropriate participation of qualified staff members in major policy decisions.		

Worksheet 8.2 (Continued)

	Column 1	Column 2
Have unfair work performance expectations.		
Inadequately compensate employees.		
Do not pay overtime for extra work.		
Take credit for staff accomplishments.		
Blame employees for their own mistakes.		
Advance their personal career instead of working in the best interest of the organization.		
Create unhealthy competition between employees.		
Give inadequate feedback or withhold information to gain or keep power to themselves.		
Cast doubt on the credibility of other managers.		
Gossip about other managers.		
Ignore company policies when they want.		
Discipline unfairly or inhumanely when discipline is warranted.		
Top Management …		
Mismanages corporate assets.		
Accepts or creates reports that distort our actual performance.		
Fails to address long-term problems.		
Fails to discipline or terminate incompetent managers.		
Pays itself in excess of its worth.		
Misallocates human resources.		
Inconsistently applies policies between staff or departments.		
Has conflicts of interest.		
Is not really living up to our mission statement.		
Service to Our Customers …		
We really care about our customers.		
We display rude or arrogant behavior to our customers.		
We say unkind things about customers when they aren't there.		
We provide an inadequate response to customer requests.		
We make offers to customers to increase sales knowing we don't have the product available or the staff to handle the needs.		
We do not make it a priority to respond to customer requests in a timely manner.		
Comments		

- Are you satisfied that the standards of behavior you have set are high enough?

- Are there items that should be added to this list that are unique to your company or industry?

- Do you have a policy and procedures manual or employee handbook that sets standards on these issues?

- Should some of these behaviors be cause for termination of employment?

WHAT'S NEXT

Now that you've considered all of the worksheets and exercises, the rest is up to you. I hope this book has given you the necessary tools for growing your business in the long term and managing your course of action day-to-day. But as we've said from the beginning, the game is not won by the plan but by the execution. Create your vision, set high standards, build long-term growth, and lead with courage. Then enjoy the results.

APPENDIX ONE

THE 50 CRITICAL MANAGEMENT QUESTIONS TO RUNNING A SUCCESSFUL BUSINESS

Throughout this book, there have been hundreds of questions essential to running a great business. Of all the questions in this book, I consider these the 50 most critical. Consider making each of these questions the topic for weekly management meetings.

1. Do we have a vision about where we are going as a company?

2. Do we plan adequately to grow the company?

3. Do we communicate the plan to all who are involved with the company?

4. Do we have good cash management?

5. Are we building cash?

6. Is the overall financial condition of the company improving or deteriorating?

7. Do we have timely and accurate financial data to review?

8. Does the data we have help you make decisions? Do we need more? Do we look at all the data you receive each month?

9. Do employees understand how their work impacts the company financially?

10. Is our company performing well compared to industry standards?

11. Do we have adequate internal controls to prevent employee theft?

12. Do we meet with employees at least once a month to review variances and trends?

13. Are we losing market share?

14. Have we surveyed or otherwise communicated with our customers for their input in improvements in service and new products?

15. Are overall customer complaints trending up or down?

16. Do we clearly understand our customers and markets?

17. Do we know where we are positioned in our market?

18. Are our products and services out of date?

19. Is our pricing appropriate and competitive?

20. Are we regularly creating new products and offering them to existing customers?

21. Are we satisfied with our revenue growth?

22. Are all of our product sales profitable?

23. Is our customer base shrinking or increasing?

24. Can we identify customers or groups of customers whose business is not profitable for us?

25. Are we satisfied with our plans to expand via the Internet?

26. Do we spend time with our direct reports, one-to-one?

27. Do we spend time with our top customers, one-to-one?

28. Are our sales and customer service people superstars?

29. Do you celebrate the achievements of the company and its employees?

30. Do we self-audit our own records and the maintenance of equipment?

31. Do we have back-up suppliers for most of our manufacturing process needs?

32. Do we have adequate internal quality controls, or are our customers the first to know if one of your processes failed?

33. Have we adequately protected our intellectual property?

34. Are our facilities that are adequate for today also adequate for our growth plans?

35. Are we adequately minimizing the threats to our business?

36. Are our facilities and information systems prepared for a natural disaster or other physically destructive force?

37. Do we have adequate back-up procedures for our information systems?

38. Are we making the best use of available new technologies in manufacturing?

39. Have we talked to our suppliers about better prices or terms or other changes to our relationship to benefit us both?

40. Do we regularly chart and review operational performance?

41. Do we spend enough time to be sure we are hiring for the long run?

42. Do we follow compliance laws and have written policies as required?

43. Are we following procedures that are most likely to keep us out of employee lawsuits?

44. Does our compensation and benefit structure allow us to hire highly talented employees?

45. Are our employees overworked? Do we spend a lot in overtime and temporary help? Is that number increasing?

46. Do we tolerate gossip or other behavior that undermines employee morale?

47. Do we ask employees to review the company?

48. Do we give enough types of feedback to employees about their performance? Do we review them individually at least annually?

49. Do we insist our employees stay employable?

50. Is the CEO accountable to someone for his or her decisions and actions? Does the board (if you have one) communicate their expectations about the company?

Appendix Two

Top 50 Practical Business Books

A library of business books will not tell you how to run your business. Only experience can do that. But you can get some good ideas that might work for you. This list is not the all-time great business books. It is instead some of the most practical books I have found. They have given me some of the best ideas that I've been able to implement to some success. I hope they work that way for you, too.

Planning

Making Success Measurable! by Douglas K. Smith.
John Wiley & Sons, 1999.

The Successful Business Plan by Rhoda Adams.
Running "R" Media, 2000.

Simplified Strategic Planning: The No-Nonsense Guide for Busy People Who Want Results by Robert W. Bradford, J. Peter Duncan, and Brian Tarcy.
Chandler House Press, 1999.

Making Sense of Strategy by Tony Manning.
AMACOM, 2002.

Plan for Profitability: How to Write a Strategic Business Plan by Lee E. Hargrave.
Four Seasons Publishers, 1999.

Budgeting

Finance for Non-Financial Managers by Herbert T. Spiro.
John Wiley & Sons, 1996.

Total Business Budgeting by Robert Rachlin.
John Wiley & Sons, 1999.

Budget Basics & Beyond by Jae K. Shim and Joel G. Siegel.
Prentice Hall Trade, 1994.

Forecasting Budgets: 25 Keys to Successful Planning
by Norman Moore and Grover Gardner.
Lebhar-Friedman Books, 1999.

The Open-Book Management Field Book by John B. Schuster, Jill Carpenter,
and Patricia Kane.
John Wiley & Sons, 1998.

Running the Numbers

The Fast Forward MBA in Finance by John Tracy.
John Wiley & Sons, 2002.

Essentials of Financial Analysis by George Friedlob and
Lydia LF Schleifer.
John Wiley & Sons, 2002.

Essentials of Cash Flow by H. A. Schaeffer.
John Wiley & Sons, 2002.

Open Book Management: The Coming Business Revolution
by John Case.
HarperCollins, 1995.

*Managing by the Numbers: A Commonsense Guide to Understanding
and Using Your Company's Financials* by Chuck Kremer, Ron Rizzuto,
and John F. Case.
Perseus Publishing, 2000.,

Sales and Customer Service

Exceptional Customer Service by Lisa Ford, David McNair, and Bill Perry. Adams Media Corporation, 2001.

Best Practices in Customer Service by Ron Zemke and John A. Woods. AMACOM, 1999.

The Nordstrom Way by Robert Spector. John Wiley & Sons, 1996.

Monitoring, Measuring & Managing Customer Service by Gary S. Goodman. Jossey-Bass, 2000.

The Accidental Salesperson: How to Take Control of Your Sales Career and Earn the Respect and Income You Deserve by Chris Lytle. AMACOM, 2000.

Operations

Execution: The Discipline of Getting Things Done by Larry Bossidy, Ram Charan, and Charles Burck. Crown Publishing, 2002.

The Circle of Innovation by Tom Peters. Random House Trade Paperbacks, 1999.

201 Great Ideas for Your Small Business by Jane Applegate. Bloomberg Press, 2002.

Driving Fear Out of the Workplace: Creating the High-Trust, High Performance Organization by Kathleen D. Ryan and Daniel K. Gestreich. Jossey-Bass, 1998.

The Black Enterprise Guide to Technology for Entrepreneurs by Bernadette Williams. John Wiley & Sons, 2001.

People Management

The Boss's Survival Guide by Bob Rosner, Allan Halcrow, and Alan S. Levins. McGraw-Hill Trade, 2001.

Managing Performance, Managing People: Understanding and Improving Team Performance by Murray Ainsworth, Neville Smith, and Anne Millership. Longman, 2001.

The Bad Attitude Survival Guide by Harry E. Chambers. Perseus Publishing, 1998.

Keeping Good People: Strategies for Solving the #1 Problem Facing Business Today by Roger E. Herman. Oakhill Press, 1999.

The Unofficial Guide to Hiring and Firing People by Alan S. Horowitz. Hungry Minds, Inc., 1999.

Personal Growth

Principle Centered Leadership by Steven Covey. Simon & Schuster, 1992.

Big Vision, Small Business by Jamie S. Walters. Berrett-Koehler Publishing, 2002.

Leap of Strength: A Personal Tour Through the Months Before and Years After You Start Your Own Business by Walter G. Sutton. Silver Lake Publishing, 2000.

Thinking for a Change: 11 Ways Highly Successful People Approach Life and Work by John C. Maxwell. Warner Books, 2003.

Fierce Conversations by Susan Scott. Viking Press, 2002.

Corporate Change and Growth

Alchemy of Growth: Practical Insights for Building the Enduring Enterprise by Merhdad Baghai, Stephen Coley, and David White. Perseus Publishing, 2000.

Leading Strategic Change by J. Stewart Black and Hal B. Gregersen. Financial Times Prentice Hall, 2002.

Managing Transitions by William Bridges. Perseus Publishing, 1991.

Strategic Action Planning Now! by Cate Gable. Saint Lucie Press, 1998.

The E-Myth Revisited: Why Most Small Businesses Don't Work and What to Do About It by Michael E. Gerber. HarperBusiness, 1995.

Leadership

On Becoming a Leader by Warren Bennis. Perseus Publishing, 1994.

Leadership Jazz by Max De Pree. Doubleday Trade Press, 1993.

Pour Your Heart Into It: How Starbucks Built a Company One Cup at a Time by Howard Schultz and Dori Jones Yang. Hyperion, 1999.

Primal Leadership: Realizing the Power of Emotional Intelligence by Daniel Goldman, Annie McKee, and Richard E. Boyatzis. Harvard Business School Press, 2002.

Built to Last: Successful Habits of Visionary Companies by Jim Collins and Jerry I. Porras. HarperCollins, 1994.

Marketing

The Marketing Toolkit for Growing Businesses by Jay B. Lipe. Chammerson Press, 2002.

Guerilla Marketing: Secrets for Making Big Profits from Your Small Business by Jay Conrad Levinson. Mariner Books, 1998.

The Anatomy of a Buzz: How to Create Word-of-Mouth Marketing by Emanuel Rosen. Doubleday, 2002.

The 22 Immutable Laws of Branding by Al Ries and Laura Ries. HarperCollins, 2002.

What Clients Love: The Field Guide to Growing Your Business by Harry Beckwith. Warner Books, 2003.

INDEX